The Passover Haggadah

Compiled by

RABBI MORRIS SILVERMAN

- *with contemporary readings,*
- *historical commentary,*
- *explanatory notes, and*
- *concise instructions.*

הגדה של פסח

NEWLY REVISED EDITION

with TRANSLITERATION
of key blessings and songs.

Edited by JONATHAN D. LEVINE

Traditional passages & page numbers compatible with earlier editions.

THE PRAYER BOOK PRESS

An affiliate of MEDIA JUDAICA

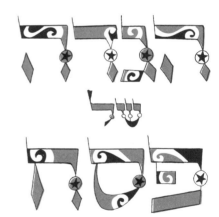

הַגָּדָה שֶׁל פֶּסַח

This Silverman Haggadah includes the *complete* traditional text, in Hebrew and in English, as well as instructions and explanatory notes for all ceremonies and Seder procedures.

Gender-sensitive language has been used for all *human* actions and references.

Commentary and Historical Notes appear on various pages throughout.

Transliterated Ceremonial Blessings & Refrains appear on various pages throughout.

Illustrated by Ezekiel Schloss

THE PRAYER BOOK PRESS of Media Judaica, Inc.

1363 Fairfield Avenue, Bridgeport, Conn. 06605

Published In Memory of ALTHEA SILVERMAN,

A "Woman of Valor," who spoke with wisdom, and taught kindness.

Library of Congress Catalog Card Number: 59-7604 / ISBN 0-87677-082-0

1997 Printing

HOW IS THIS HAGGADAH DIFFERENT?

(And how can it enhance your Seder?)

The joyous celebration of the Passover Seder is one of the most beautiful and meaningful occasions of the Jewish year. This Haggadah is designed to enable everyone attending to *understand* and to *enjoy* the Seder—and to *participate* in it, with comfort and ease.

This Haggadah is both traditional and modern. It provides historical commentary as it explains the ceremonies; and it interprets ancient traditions in a modern spirit. Using *contemporary* and *classical* sources, it illustrates the enduring relevance of Pesaḥ. And all of this is done *concisely*—without overwhelming the participants, and without unduly lengthening the Seder service.

By identifying essential portions of the traditional Haggadah (in larger print) and by providing easy-to-follow instructions, explanatory notes, and extensive transliteration, we hope to encourage *meaningful* participation.

Optional readings are placed below a "dividing line" on certain pages —or in brackets or smaller print on other pages. Thus identified, they can be used *selectively*. While the *complete* Hebrew text is provided, several less essential portions of the Hebrew text appear in smaller print; others are preceded by notes suggesting selective choices (perhaps for alternate Seder nights).

The traditional Haggadah is a unique document, incorporating Jewish history, literature, folklore, and song. Some of its texts and rituals are ancient, linked to observances in Jerusalem more than two thousand years ago. Some selections were added in the eighth and ninth centuries; others as late as the fifteenth century.

This edition continues the Haggadah's development; it introduces prayers and readings reflecting events in our own century—among them the Holocaust, the rebirth of the State of Israel, and the universal quest for justice and freedom. (The original "Silverman Haggadah" was the first traditional Haggadah to utilize this approach.) Interpretive captions now precede many traditional passages.

We suggest that *favorite poems, readings, and quotations be brought to the Seder*, to be read by participants, thus bridging the generations and amplifying the themes of Pesaḥ in a personal way. (See p. vi) Favorite melodies will also enliven the Seder.

In addition to its historical and religious significance, the Seder has become, in our day, an important opportunity for Jewish self-affirmation. In spirit, format, and content, our Haggadah strives to enhance this splendid occasion.

RABBI JONATHAN D. LEVINE

PREPARATION AND CELEBRATION

Even the most experienced Seder Leader should review this Haggadah *in advance*. The Leader should be prepared to: recite several traditional portions of the text, *explain* and coordinate the service, and perhaps also lead the singing of the main Seder melodies (or "cue" the person who will lead the singing).

Since last-minute choices of passages to be recited rarely yield a balanced Seder, the Leader should select, *in advance*, some of the explanatory notes to be discussed and some contemporary readings to be recited. From among these (and from the traditional text) several passages should be assigned for recitation by others. Children may be invited to read or chant passages learned in school.

Whenever possible, Hebrew passages should be chanted or sung. Here too, advance preparation will be helpful—for instance, in determining which melodies are familiar to those attending, and which new melodies are to be introduced. Individual participants may be invited to chant a passage—or to teach a melody known to some but not to others.

In a group of various backgrounds, particular attention should be given to the transliterated blessings and songs—which should be announced by the Leader.

Questions and discussion should be encouraged—but the constraints of time should be kept in mind, so that the *balance* of the Seder is not indiscriminately rushed. (Abbreviations should be *planned in advance!*)

VIVID AND VISUAL EXPERIENCES

Much of the *visual* impact of the Seder is created by the ceremonial objects; but special decorations can add immeasurably to the holiday atmosphere and can highlight the festival themes, whose expression need not be limited to words.

Preparing decorations for the Seder table, for the Seder room, and even for the home, can be a meaningful family project *before* the Seder—and will add to the festival spirit *during* the Seder. Place cards may be decorated with Passover symbols or Spring motifs. A Matzah Cover may be embroidered, etc.

Guests too may be invited to bring decorations. As with the "bringing" of favorite quotations or poems to be shared at the Seder, preparing or bringing decorations is yet another opportunity for *involvement* on Passover night.

As part of the pageantry of the evening, the host or the Leader may wear a white robe (known as a *kittel*) which is a reminder of the vestment worn on sacred occasions by the priests in the ancient Temple. (White is a symbol of festivity, purity, and freedom.) Here too opportunities for *pre*-holiday projects abound. A kittel may be designed, sewn, and even decorated; a kippah may be made and decorated, for one's self or for a loved one, and used on Pesaḥ.*

A novel visual suggestion: Objects of historic or personal Jewish interest may be "on display" during Passover—including books, photographs, ceremonial objects, memorabilia. And *one* way of distinguishing one Seder from another is to vary the "conversation pieces" placed on display!

---

* On the left side of the Leader's armchair (optionally for others) one or two pillows are placed for "reclining" while reciting certain parts of the service. (See page 10.) Special "reclining pillows" may be sewn and decorated for this occasion.

THE SEDER TABLE

The Seder table should be attractively set. Spring flowers are particularly appropriate. (Pesaḥ is called *Ḥag Ha-Aviv*, Festival of Spring.) Place candlesticks on the table or nearby.

Candles are kindled just before the Meditation and Blessings which appear on page X.

At the head of the table are: the "Ceremonial Plate," the Leader's Kiddush cup, a decanter of wine, a bowl of salt water, and three matzot placed one on top of the other (in a cloth matzah cover, or in a wooden or silver matzah tier).

A large wine cup is placed in the center of the table, as the "Cup of Elijah."

Each person is provided with a Haggadah, a Kiddush cup, a *kipah*, and a small dish (not the dinner plate) for ceremonial foods and salt water.

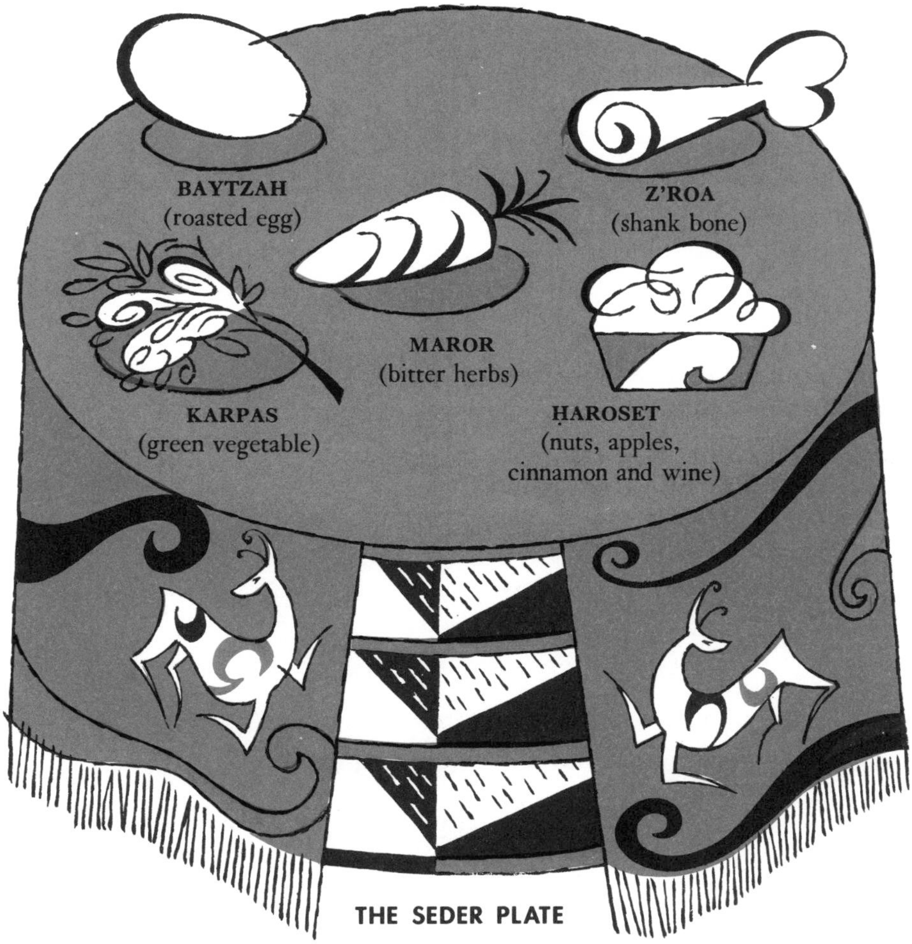

THE SEDER PLATE

The Ceremonial Seder Plate contains: (1) a charred shank bone of lamb (*Z'roa*); (2) a roasted egg (*Baytzah*); (3) bitter herbs (*Maror*), *i.e.* horseradish; (4) greens, such as parsley or celery (*Karpas*); (5) a mixture of grated nuts, grated apples, cinnamon, and wine (*Ḥaroset*).

(A dish of *grated* horseradish may be used for the second *Maror*.)

A Practical Suggestion

To accelerate distribution of the ceremonial foods and the filling of the four cups of wine (especially when there are many guests present), *duplicate* "ceremonial plates," wine bottles, salt water containers, *Ḥaroset* and *Maror* bowls, etc., may be strategically placed around the table.

Optional: A pitcher of water, with bowl or basin, may be placed near the table, for the ceremonial washing of hands. (See page 5.)

A Note on Matzah and Ḥametz

According to traditional sources, when the Israelites left Egypt hastily, they had no time to bake regular bread with leaven (*Ḥametz*). As a commemoration, unleavened bread (*Matzah*) is used during Passover. In accordance with the command "No leaven shall be seen in your home" (Exodus 13:7), Jewish homes are cleansed of all *Ḥametz* before Pesaḥ. (Thus, "spring housecleaning" has become part of the Passover tradition.)

For guidance on removal of Ḥametz *(foods and other items) from the home, consult your rabbi.*

BEDIKAT ḤAMETZ: Ceremony of Removing the Leaven

The ceremonial cleansing of the home culminates with the ancient and colorful ceremony of searching for the leaven (*Bedikat Ḥametz*) and removing it (*Biur Ḥametz*) on the night before the night of the first Seder.

By candlelight, (and using a feather and a wooden or paper bowl) parents and children go from room to room "searching for" and collecting crumbs of bread (previously placed where they may be easily found). Crumbs and bowl are then wrapped together, the declaration "May all leaven . . ." is recited, and they are burned on the following morning.

On the evening before the night of the first Seder (on Thursday night when the first day of Passover occurs on Sunday), the search for leaven begins with the following blessing:

Praised be Thou, O Lord our God, King of the universe, who hast sanctified us with Thy commandments and enjoined upon us the mitzvah of removing leaven before Passover.

בָּרוּךְ אַתָּה, יְיָ אֱלֹהֵינוּ, מֶלֶךְ הָעוֹלָם, אֲשֶׁר קִדְּשָׁנוּ בְּמִצְוֹתָיו, וְצִוָּנוּ עַל בִּעוּר חָמֵץ.

After the search, wrap the leaven and receptacle together and recite this declaration:

May all leaven in my possession which I have not seen or removed, be regarded as non-existent and considered as mere dust of the earth.

כָּל חֲמִירָא וַחֲמִיעָא דְּאִכָּא בִרְשׁוּתִי, דְּלָא חֲמִתֵּהּ וּדְלָא בִעַרְתֵּהּ, וּדְלָא יְדַעְנָא לֵהּ, לִבָּטֵל וְלֶהֱוֵי הֶפְקֵר כְּעַפְרָא דְאַרְעָא.

The following morning after breakfast (on Friday morning if the first day of Pesaḥ is Sunday), the leaven is burned, and the following final declaration is recited:

May all leaven in my possession, whether I have seen it or not, or whether I have removed it or not, be regarded as non-existent and considered as mere dust of the earth.

כָּל חֲמִירָא וַחֲמִיעָא דְּאִכָּא בִרְשׁוּתִי, דַּחֲזִתֵּהּ וּדְלָא חֲזִיתֵּהּ, דַּחֲמִתֵּהּ וּדְלָא חֲמִתֵּהּ, דְּבִעַרְתֵּהּ וּדְלָא בִעַרְתֵּהּ, לִבָּטֵל וְלֶהֱוֵי הֶפְקֵר כְּעַפְרָא דְאַרְעָא.

ORDER OF THE SERVICE

קדש

1. Kaddesh —
SANCTIFY THE NAME OF GOD.

ורחץ

2. U-r'ḥatz —
WASH THE HANDS.

כרפס

3. Karpas —
EAT A GREEN VEGETABLE.

יחץ

4. Yaḥatz —
BREAK THE MIDDLE OF THE THREE MATZOT.

מגיד

5. Maggid —
TELL THE STORY OF THE EXODUS.

רחצה

6. Raḥatz —
WASH THE HANDS BEFORE THE MEAL.

מוציא

7. Motzi —
SAY THE HA-MOTZI.

מצה

8. Matzah —
RECITE THE BLESSING FOR THE MATZAH.

מרור

9. Maror —
EAT THE BITTER HERBS.

כורך

10. Korekh —
EAT THE MATZAH AND MAROR SANDWICH.

שלחן עורך

11. Shulḥan Orekh — ENJOY THE FESTIVAL MEAL.

צפון

12. Tzafun —
EAT THE AFIKOMAN.

ברך

13. Barekh —
SAY THE BLESSING AFTER THE MEAL.

הלל

14. Hallel —
RECITE THE HALLEL.

נרצה

15. Nirtzah —
CONCLUDE THE SEDER.

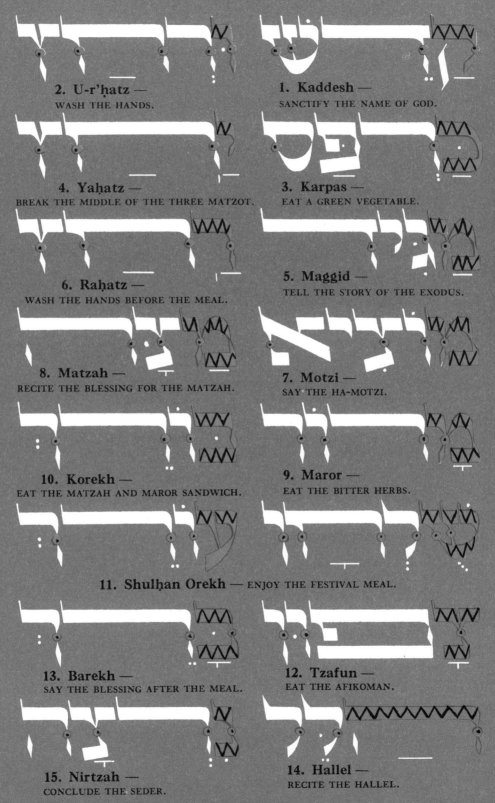

KINDLING THE FESTIVAL CANDLES

Before sunset and prior to the Seder, light candles and recite:

Our God and God of our ancestors, may the rays of these festival candles cast their glow upon the earth and bring the radiance of Thy divine light to all who still dwell in darkness and in bondage. May this season, marking the deliverance of our ancestors from Pharaoh, arouse us against any despot who keeps others bowed in servitude. In gratitude for the freedom which is ours, may we strive to bring about the liberation of all. Bless our home and our dear ones with the light of Thy spirit. Amen.

On Sabbath add words in brackets.

Praised be Thou, O Lord our God, King of the universe, who hast sanctified us with Thy commandments, and enjoined upon us the mitzvah of kindling the [Sabbath and the] Festival lights.

בָּרוּךְ אַתָּה, יְיָ אֱלֹהֵינוּ, מֶלֶךְ
הָעוֹלָם, אֲשֶׁר קִדְּשָׁנוּ בְּמִצְוֹתָיו וְצִוָּנוּ
לְהַדְלִיק נֵר שֶׁל [שַׁבָּת וְשֶׁל] יוֹם טוֹב.

Baruḥ atta Adonai, eloheynu meleḥ ha-olam, asher kid-shanu b'mitzvo-tav, ve-tzivanu le-hadlik nayr shel [shabbat ve-shel] yom tov.

Praised be Thou, O Lord our God, King of the universe, who hast kept us in life and sustained us, and enabled us to reach this season.

בָּרוּךְ אַתָּה, יְיָ אֱלֹהֵינוּ, מֶלֶךְ
הָעוֹלָם, שֶׁהֶחֱיָנוּ וְקִיְּמָנוּ וְהִגִּיעָנוּ לַזְּמַן
הַזֶּה.

Baruḥ atta Adonai, eloheynu meleḥ ha-olam,
she-he-ḥe-yanu, ve-kiy'manu, ve-higi-anu la-z'man ha-zeh.

Parental Blessing

For sons:

May God bless you as He blessed Ephraim and Manasseh.

יְשִׂמְךָ אֱלֹהִים כְּאֶפְרַיִם וְכִמְנַשֶּׁה.

For daughters:

May God bless you as He blessed Sarah, Rebecca, Rachel and Leah.

יְשִׂמֵךְ אֱלֹהִים כְּשָׂרָה, רִבְקָה
רָחֵל וְלֵאָה.

Y'VAREḤEḤA — The Threefold Blessing

Recite the following for all assembled:

May God bless you and keep you;
May God cause His spirit to shine upon you and be gracious unto you;
May God turn His spirit unto you and grant you peace.

יְבָרֶכְךָ יְיָ וְיִשְׁמְרֶךָ.

יָאֵר יְיָ פָּנָיו אֵלֶיךָ וִיחֻנֶּךָּ.

יִשָּׂא יְיָ פָּנָיו אֵלֶיךָ וְיָשֵׂם לְךָ שָׁלוֹם.

The name HAGGADAH *means "the telling," reflecting the Biblical Command: "You shall tell" the story of the liberation from bondage (Exodus 13:8).*

The word SEDER *means Order: the prescribed "Order of the Observance" (see below).*

קדש ורחץ

"KADDESH U-R'ḤATZ": The Order of the Service

(The Fifteen Steps of the Seder)

1.	Sanctify (Recite the Kiddush)	*Kaddesh*	קַדֵּשׁ
2.	Wash the Hands	*U-r'ḥatz*	וּרְחַץ
3.	Eat the Green Vegetable	*Karpas*	כַּרְפַּס
4.	Break the Middle of Three Matzot	*Yaḥatz*	יַחַץ
5.	Tell the Story of the Exodus	*Maggid*	מַגִּיד
6.	Wash Hands Before the Meal	*Raḥtza*	רָחְצָה
7.	Say Ha-Motzi	*Motzi*	מוֹצִיא
8.	Recite Blessing for the Matzah	*Matzah*	מַצָּה
9.	Eat Bitter Herbs (Dipped in Ḥaroset)	*Maror*	מָרוֹר
10.	Eat Matzah and Maror Sandwich	*Korekh*	כּוֹרֵךְ
11.	Enjoy the Festival Meal	*Shulḥan Orekh*	שֻׁלְחָן עוֹרֵךְ
12.	Eat the Afikoman	*Tzafun*	צָפוּן
13.	Recite Birkat Hamazon (Grace)	*Barekh*	בָּרֵךְ
14.	Recite the Hallel (Second Part)	*Hallel*	הַלֵּל
15.	Conclude the Seder	*Nirtzah*	נִרְצָה

"Kaddesh U-r'ḥatz," intended as a convenient outline of the traditional Seder service, was compiled as a mnemonic rhyme (perhaps by Rashi, or one of his students, in eleventh-century France). The basic structure of the Seder originated in the period of the Mishnah. In subsequent generations, the Haggadah, a unique document of history, ritual, law, and lore, developed in many forms; liturgical, artistic, and ceremonial variations abound—traditionally and in our own day.

The "Kaddesh U-r'ḥatz" Outline, often chanted or sung as a "prelude" to the Seder, highlights the *unity* among the various rites.

שָׁלוֹם

THE MESSAGE OF PASSOVER

Introductory Reading

Welcome to our Seder! Tonight we observe an ancient, colorful, and significant Festival. The Seder takes us back to events which occurred more than three thousand years ago, as we recall the bondage of the Children of Israel and their deliverance.

History tells us that many other peoples were also enslaved by tyrants. But the Israelites were the first to rebel against serfdom, and to institute a holiday dedicated to freedom.

Most nations observe an Independence Day; but the observance of the birthday of Jewish freedom is unique because of its profoundly religious character and forms. Every Jewish home becomes a sanctuary, every table an altar where gratitude is expressed to God, the Author of liberty. Through prayer and song, ritual and symbol, custom and ceremony, we fulfill the command to "look upon ourselves as though *we* were among those enslaved and then brought forth unto freedom."

This self-identification with the past of our people helps us to appreciate the freedom that is ours—and to understand more fully the plight of those of our people who still dwell under the shadow of tyranny. The Seder calls upon us to do all in our power to emancipate them from oppression.

The Seder, which emphasizes love of liberty, has significance for all people. Freedom, one of our most precious gifts, must not be taken for granted. In every age it must be won anew. The Pharaoh of the Exodus is symbolic of tyrants in every era of history.

If a people is anywhere exploited and oppressed, then nowhere is freedom really secure. The Seder summons us to vigilance in the struggle to preserve and advance the cause of freedom and human dignity. May true freedom soon become the lot of all God's children!

1. Kaddesh — Sanctify (Recite the Kiddush) — קַדֵּשׁ

Fill the first cup of wine.

Leader

We begin our service by sanctifying the name of God and proclaiming the sanctity of this Festival. With a blessing over wine, we Jews usher in the Sabbath and all Festivals. And so, with a cup of wine, symbol of joy, let us now welcome the Festival of Passover.

We Dedicate This Night...

In unison

Our God and God of our ancestors, we thank Thee that Thou hast enabled us to gather in happy fellowship, again to observe the Festival of Freedom. Just as for many centuries the Seder has brought together families and friends to retell the events which led to our freedom, so may we this night be at one with Jews everywhere who perform this ancient ritual linking us with our historic past. As we relive each event in our people's ancient struggle, and celebrate their emergence from slavery to freedom, we pray that all of us may keep alive in our hearts the love of liberty. May we dedicate our lives to the abolition of all forms of tyranny and injustice.

Leader

As we partake of this cup of wine, we acknowledge Thee as our Creator and Liberator, and praise Thy holy name in the traditional words of the Kiddush:

On Sabbath add this paragraph:
(On other nights, the Kiddush begins with the blessing below.)

וַיְהִי עֶרֶב וַיְהִי בֹקֶר

יוֹם הַשִּׁשִּׁי. וַיְכֻלּוּ הַשָּׁמַיִם וְהָאָרֶץ וְכָל צְבָאָם. וַיְכַל אֱלֹהִים בַּיּוֹם הַשְּׁבִיעִי מְלַאכְתּוֹ אֲשֶׁר עָשָׂה, וַיִּשְׁבֹּת בַּיּוֹם הַשְּׁבִיעִי מִכָּל מְלַאכְתּוֹ אֲשֶׁר עָשָׂה. וַיְבָרֶךְ אֱלֹהִים אֶת יוֹם הַשְּׁבִיעִי וַיְקַדֵּשׁ אֹתוֹ, כִּי בוֹ שָׁבַת מִכָּל מְלַאכְתּוֹ אֲשֶׁר בָּרָא אֱלֹהִים לַעֲשׂוֹת.

And there was evening and there was morning — the sixth day. Now the heavens and the earth — yea, the whole universe — were finished. And by the seventh day God had finished the work which He had done; and on the seventh day He ceased from all the work which He had done. Then God blessed the seventh day and hallowed it, for on it He rested from all the work which, in creating, He had done. (Gen. 1:31–2:3)

בָּרוּךְ אַתָּה יְיָ אֱלֹהֵינוּ מֶלֶךְ הָעוֹלָם בּוֹרֵא פְּרִי הַגָּפֶן:

בָּרוּךְ אַתָּה, יְיָ אֱלֹהֵינוּ, מֶלֶךְ הָעוֹלָם, בּוֹרֵא פְּרִי הַגָּפֶן.

Baruḥ atta Adonai, eloheynu meleḥ ha-olam, boray p'ri ha-gafen.

Praised be Thou, O Lord our God, King of the Universe,
Creator of the Fruit of the Vine.

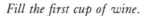

On Sabbath add words in brackets:

Praised be Thou, O Lord our God, King of the universe, who didst choose us from among all people for Thy service, and exalted us by teaching us holiness through Thy commandments. Out of love hast Thou given us, O Lord our God, [Sabbaths for rest,] holidays for gladness, festivals and seasons for rejoicing, among them [this Sabbath day and] this day of the Feast of Unleavened Bread, the season of our freedom, a festival of holy assembly, commemorating our liberation from Egypt. From among all peoples hast Thou chosen us, and didst sanctify us by giving us Thy holy [Sabbath and] Festivals as a joyous heritage. Praised be Thou, O Lord, who hallowest [the Sabbath,] Israel and the Festivals.

בָּרוּךְ אַתָּה, יְיָ אֱלֹהֵינוּ, מֶלֶךְ הָעוֹלָם, אֲשֶׁר בָּחַר בָּנוּ מִכָּל עָם, וְרוֹמְמָנוּ מִכָּל לָשׁוֹן, וְקִדְּשָׁנוּ בְּמִצְוֹתָיו. וַתִּתֶּן־לָנוּ, יְיָ אֱלֹהֵינוּ, בְּאַהֲבָה [שַׁבָּתוֹת לִמְנוּחָה וּ]מוֹעֲדִים לְשִׂמְחָה, חַגִּים וּזְמַנִּים לְשָׂשׂוֹן, אֶת יוֹם [הַשַּׁבָּת הַזֶּה, וְאֶת יוֹם] חַג הַמַּצּוֹת הַזֶּה, זְמַן חֵרוּתֵנוּ, [בְּאַהֲבָה] מִקְרָא קֹדֶשׁ, זֵכֶר לִיצִיאַת מִצְרָיִם. כִּי בָנוּ בָחַרְתָּ, וְאוֹתָנוּ קִדַּשְׁתָּ מִכָּל הָעַמִּים, [וְשַׁבָּת] וּמוֹעֲדֵי קָדְשְׁךָ [בְּאַהֲבָה וּבְרָצוֹן] בְּשִׂמְחָה וּבְשָׂשׂוֹן הִנְחַלְתָּנוּ. בָּרוּךְ אַתָּה, יְיָ, מְקַדֵּשׁ [הַשַּׁבָּת וְ]יִשְׂרָאֵל וְהַזְּמַנִּים.

On Saturday night continue with HAVDALAH *(below).*
On other nights continue with SHE-HE-ḤE-YA-NU *(next page).*

Havdalah

Praised be Thou, O Lord our God, King of the universe, Creator of the light of fire.

בָּרוּךְ אַתָּה, יְיָ אֱלֹהֵינוּ, מֶלֶךְ הָעוֹלָם, בּוֹרֵא מְאוֹרֵי הָאֵשׁ.

Praised be Thou, O Lord our God, King of the universe, who makest a distinction between the sacred and the secular, between light and darkness, between Israel and the heathen, between the seventh day of rest and the six days of work. Thou hast made a distinction between the higher sanctity of the Sabbath and the lesser sanctity of the Festival, and hast hallowed the Sabbath above the six days of work. Thus hast Thou distinguished and sanctified Israel with Thine own sanctity. Praised be Thou, O Lord, who distinguishest between the sanctity of the Sabbath and the sanctity of the Festivals.

בָּרוּךְ אַתָּה, יְיָ אֱלֹהֵינוּ, מֶלֶךְ הָעוֹלָם, הַמַּבְדִּיל בֵּין קֹדֶשׁ לְחֹל, בֵּין אוֹר לְחֹשֶׁךְ, בֵּין יִשְׂרָאֵל לָעַמִּים, בֵּין יוֹם הַשְּׁבִיעִי לְשֵׁשֶׁת יְמֵי הַמַּעֲשֶׂה. בֵּין קְדֻשַּׁת שַׁבָּת לִקְדֻשַּׁת יוֹם טוֹב הִבְדַּלְתָּ, וְאֶת יוֹם הַשְּׁבִיעִי מִשֵּׁשֶׁת יְמֵי הַמַּעֲשֶׂה קִדַּשְׁתָּ; הִבְדַּלְתָּ וְקִדַּשְׁתָּ אֶת עַמְּךָ יִשְׂרָאֵל בִּקְדֻשָּׁתֶךָ. בָּרוּךְ אַתָּה, יְיָ, הַמַּבְדִּיל בֵּין קֹדֶשׁ לְקֹדֶשׁ.

She-he-ḥe-ya-nu (Blessing of Thanksgiving)

בָּרוּךְ אַתָּה, יְיָ אֱלֹהֵינוּ, מֶלֶךְ הָעוֹלָם, שֶׁהֶחֱיָנוּ וְקִיְּמָנוּ וְהִגִּיעָנוּ לַזְּמַן הַזֶּה.

Baruḥ atta Adonai, eloheynu meleḥ ha-olam,
she-he-ḥe-yanu, ve-kiy'manu, ve-higi-anu la-z'man ha-zeh.

Praised be Thou, O Lord our God, King of the Universe, Who hast Kept Us in Life and Sustained Us, and Enabled Us to Reach this Season.

While reclining to the left, drink the first cup of wine.

2. U-r'ḥatz — Wash the Hands

Since HAMOTZI (the blessing for bread preceding the meal) does not follow at this point, the usual blessing for washing the hands is omitted.

(A pitcher of water, with basin and towels, my be set at a convenient place near the table. Alternatively, three participants may be delegated to leave the table for washing of hands.)

3. Karpas — Eat a Green Vegetable

The Haggadah preserves some of the customs extant when the Temple was still in existence in Jerusalem. All formal dinners began with an hors d'oeuvre. KARPAS is the hors d'oeuvre or appetizer of the Passover meal. It may consist of any green vegetable: parsley, lettuce, endive, cress, chervil, or scallion.

The green vegetable is a symbol of springtime and of the miracle of nature's renewal. At this season, when Mother Earth arrays herself in fresh verdure, the human spirit rises, and we renew our faith in a world where freedom and justice will prevail.

The salt water into which the KARPAS is dipped to make it palatable, has been interpreted as salty tears to remind us of the tears shed by the oppressed Israelites.

Before partaking of the KARPAS, recite the following blessing:

בָּרוּךְ אַתָּה, יְיָ אֱלֹהֵינוּ, מֶלֶךְ הָעוֹלָם, בּוֹרֵא פְּרִי הָאֲדָמָה.

Baruḥ atta Adonai, eloheynu meleḥ ha-olam, boray p'ri ha-adamah.

Praised Be Thou, O Lord our God, King of the Universe, Creator of the Fruit of the Earth.

4. Yaḥatz — Break the Middle of the Three Matzot יחץ

For the daily meal, there is one loaf of bread; but on the Sabbath there are two loaves, as a reminder of the double portion of manna which fell on Friday for the Children of Israel as they traveled in the wilderness. (Ex. 16:22) In honor of Passover, a third matzah was added—specifically for the Seder.*

The middle matzah is broken into two pieces.
The smaller piece is replaced on the Seder plate, to be used later for the HA-MOTZI.
The larger piece is wrapped in a napkin, as a symbol of the unleavened dough carried by our ancestors, to be eaten as the AFIKOMAN *at the end of the meal.*

Anyone finding the AFIKOMAN *may hide it, and later claim a reward before returning it. (The meal cannot be ritually completed without the* AFIKOMAN.)

5. Maggid — Tell the Story of the Exodus מגיד

Hospitality is a time-honored virtue among our people. The custom of inviting those who are hungry to the Seder originated in Babylonia. Therefore this "invitation" appears not in Hebrew but in Aramaic, the language then current. For our Seder to be true to tradition, we must offer hospitality to the strangers in our midst, and make it possible for the needy to observe the Seder.**

Mindful of our people's long years of persecution and wandering, we renew our commitment to the rebuilding of Zion, so that our people shall never again be homeless, and shall be assured the opportunity to live in dignity and freedom.

As we celebrate our Seder in freedom, we pray for the day when *all* shall be free—free from poverty, free from fear, free from bigotry, and free from the ravages of war.

---

* Recalling the three classifications of Jews in ancient Judea, the uppermost matzah is called KOHEN; the middle one, LEVI; and the third, YISRAEL.

When the Temple was in existence, special food, considered sacred, was eaten by the KOHANIM and the L'VI-YIM. But Passover indicates that *all* Jews are united in a covenant of equality. To demonstrate this, *everyone* at the Seder will tonight partake of all three matzot.

** Hence the importance of participating in the "MA-OT ḤITTIM Passover Fund," which supplies Passover food and wine to the poor—in one's local community and in other lands.

As a sign of hospitality, the door is opened.

The Leader uncovers the matzah, lifts up the ceremonial plate, and says:

הא לַחְמָא עַנְיָא דִּי אֲכַלוּ אַבְהָתָנָא בְּאַרְעָא דְמִצְרָיִם.

Behold the MATZAH, bread of poverty, which our ancestors ate in the land of Egypt.

כָּל דִּכְפִין יֵיתֵי וְיֵיכֻל,
כָּל דִּצְרִיךְ יֵיתֵי וְיִפְסַח.

Let all who are hungry come and eat. Let all who are needy, come and celebrate Passover with us.

הָשַׁתָּא הָכָא,
לַשָּׁנָה הַבָּאָה בְּאַרְעָא דְיִשְׂרָאֵל.

Now we are here; next year may we observe Passover in the Land of Israel.

הָשַׁתָּא עַבְדֵי,
לַשָּׁנָה הַבָּאָה בְּנֵי חוֹרִין.

Now many are still enslaved; next year may all be truly free.

Ha laḥma anya, di aḥalu avhatana, b'ara d'mitzrayim.
Kol diḥfin yai-tai ve-yai-ḥul
kol ditzriḥ yai-tai ve-yifsaḥ.
Ha-shata haḥa
leshanah haba-a
be-ara d'yisra-el.
Ha-shata avdai
leshanah haba-a
b'nai ḥorin.

(The Haggadah, the dramatic portrayal of the Exodus from Egyptian bondage, is intended for the entire family; it encourages children to ask questions concerning the rituals and the meaning of the service. The Seder brings families and friends together and strengthens the bonds of Jewish solidarity.)

After the door has been closed, the wine cup is filled for the second time. The youngest child, or a guest, asks the Four Questions.

אַרְבַּע הַקֻּשְׁיוֹת

THE FOUR QUESTIONS

Why is this night different from all other nights?

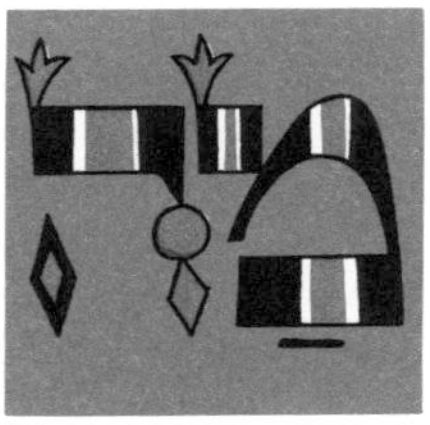

נִשְׁתַּנָּה הַלַּיְלָה הַזֶּה מִכָּל הַלֵּילוֹת?

(1) On all other nights we may eat either leavened or unleavened bread, but on this night, only unleavened bread.

(1) שֶׁבְּכָל הַלֵּילוֹת אָנוּ אוֹכְלִין חָמֵץ וּמַצָּה, הַלַּיְלָה הַזֶּה כֻּלּוֹ מַצָּה.

(2) On all other nights we eat all kinds of herbs, but on this night we eat especially bitter herbs.

(2) שֶׁבְּכָל הַלֵּילוֹת אָנוּ אוֹכְלִין שְׁאָר יְרָקוֹת, הַלַּיְלָה הַזֶּה מָרוֹר.

(3) On all other nights, we need not even once dip our herbs in any condiment, but on this night we dip herbs twice: one herb in salt water, and the bitter herbs in ḤAROSET.

(3) שֶׁבְּכָל הַלֵּילוֹת אֵין אָנוּ מַטְבִּילִין אֲפִילוּ פַּעַם אֶחָת, הַלַּיְלָה הַזֶּה שְׁתֵּי פְעָמִים.

(4) On all other nights we eat either sitting or reclining, but on this night we recline.

(4) שֶׁבְּכָל הַלֵּילוֹת אָנוּ אוֹכְלִין בֵּין יוֹשְׁבִין וּבֵין מְסֻבִּין, הַלַּיְלָה הַזֶּה כֻּלָּנוּ מְסֻבִּין.

Leader's Response to the Four Questions

Before we read the Haggadah, which recalls many aspects of the Passover story, let me answer your questions briefly:

(1) *We eat matzah* because, when our ancestors were about to leave Egypt, they had no time to bake bread with leavening; so they baked it without leaven.

(2) *We eat bitter herbs* to remind us of the bitterness our ancestors experienced when they were oppressed by their Egyptian taskmasters.

(3) *We dip food twice:* the parsley in salt water, as we have already explained, and the bitter herbs in ḤAROSET, as we shall later explain.

(4) *We lean* when we partake of wine and symbolic foods as a sign of freedom. In antiquity, slaves often ate hurriedly, standing or squatting—while royalty, nobility, and the wealthy in Egypt, Persia, Rome, and other empires, dined on couches. To indicate that the ancient Israelites were now free, they too "reclined" while eating.

(Since it is impractical for each person to have a dining couch, the Leader uses a pillow on which to lean, while others just lean when partaking of the ceremonial wine and matzah.)

FROM HUMBLE ORIGINS TO PESAḤ THANKSGIVING

Now let us return to the text of the Haggadah for the details as to why this night is different from all other nights. Whereas there are those who would like to conceal and forget their lowly origin, we Jews are constantly reminded of it. Not only at the Seder, but when we chant the Kiddush on Sabbaths and Festivals, when we read the Ten Commandments, and especially when we say our daily prayers, we recall that our ancestors were slaves in Egypt and were liberated by God. This constant reminder makes us cognizant that God works not only through nature but through history. It helps us to appreciate the importance of freedom and impresses upon us our responsibility to strive for the freedom of all.

We were once the slaves of Pharaoh in Egypt, but the Lord our God brought us forth from there with a mighty hand and an outstretched arm. (Deut. 6:21; 26:8) Had not the Holy One, praised be He, brought our ancestors out of Egypt, then we and our children and our children's children might still be enslaved to a Pharaoh in Egypt. Therefore, even if all of us were endowed with wisdom and understanding, and all of us thoroughly versed in the Torah, it would nevertheless be our duty to tell of the exodus from Egypt. And to dwell at length on the story of this liberation is indeed praiseworthy.

בָדִים הָיִינוּ לְפַרְעֹה בְּמִצְרָיִם, וַיּוֹצִיאֵנוּ יְיָ אֱלֹהֵינוּ מִשָּׁם בְּיָד חֲזָקָה וּבִזְרוֹעַ נְטוּיָה. וְאִלּוּ לֹא הוֹצִיא הַקָּדוֹשׁ בָּרוּךְ הוּא אֶת אֲבוֹתֵינוּ מִמִּצְרַיִם, הֲרֵי אָנוּ וּבָנֵינוּ, וּבְנֵי בָנֵינוּ, מְשֻׁעְבָּדִים הָיִינוּ לְפַרְעֹה בְּמִצְרָיִם. וַאֲפִילוּ כֻּלָּנוּ חֲכָמִים, כֻּלָּנוּ נְבוֹנִים, כֻּלָּנוּ זְקֵנִים, כֻּלָּנוּ יוֹדְעִים אֶת הַתּוֹרָה, מִצְוָה עָלֵינוּ לְסַפֵּר בִּיצִיאַת מִצְרָיִם. וְכָל הַמַּרְבֶּה לְסַפֵּר בִּיצִיאַת מִצְרַיִם הֲרֵי זֶה מְשֻׁבָּח.

Avadim ha-yinu . . . atta b'nai ḥorin. עֲבָדִים הָיִינוּ... עַתָּה בְּנֵי חוֹרִין.

DISCUSSIONS THROUGH THE NIGHT

The following story, for which the Haggadah is the only source, tells of a discussion by five Talmudic scholars of old – among whom was the great Rabbi Akiba. (If only we had a transcript of that night-long discussion!)*

We are told that Rabbi Eliezer, Rabbi Joshua, Rabbi Elazar, son of Azariah, Rabbi Akiba, and Rabbi Tarfon sat at the Seder table in B'nai B'rak and, the whole night through, discussed the liberation from Egypt until their disciples came in and said: "Rabbis! It is now time to recite the SHEMA of the morning prayers."

מַעֲשֶׂה בְּרַבִּי אֱלִיעֶזֶר וְרַבִּי יְהוֹשֻׁעַ, וְרַבִּי אֶלְעָזָר בֶּן עֲזַרְיָה וְרַבִּי עֲקִיבָא וְרַבִּי טַרְפוֹן, שֶׁהָיוּ מְסֻבִּין בִּבְנֵי בְרַק, וְהָיוּ מְסַפְּרִים בִּיצִיאַת מִצְרַיִם כָּל אוֹתוֹ הַלַּיְלָה, עַד שֶׁבָּאוּ תַלְמִידֵיהֶם וְאָמְרוּ לָהֶם: רַבּוֹתֵינוּ, הִגִּיעַ זְמַן קְרִיאַת שְׁמַע שֶׁל שַׁחֲרִית.

If great scholars could find discussion of the Seder so fascinating that it kept them up all night, we hope that our Seder too will be enhanced by questions and discussion.

The Haggadah text incorporates elements of discussions by the Sages over the generations. This is illustrated by the following passages.

Rabbi Elazar, son of Azariah, said, "I am nearly seventy years old, yet I never could understand why the exodus from Egypt should also be mentioned in the evening service, until Ben Zoma explained it by quoting the verse: 'That you may remember the day you went forth from Egypt all the days of your life. (Deut. 16:3) The days of your life would imply the daytime only. *All* the days of your life, includes the nights also.' " There is, however, another explanation given by the Sages: "The days of your life refers to this world. *All* the days of your life includes also the Messianic era."

אָמַר רַבִּי אֶלְעָזָר בֶּן עֲזַרְיָה: הֲרֵי אֲנִי כְּבֶן שִׁבְעִים שָׁנָה, וְלֹא זָכִיתִי שֶׁתֵּאָמֵר יְצִיאַת מִצְרַיִם בַּלֵּילוֹת, עַד שֶׁדְּרָשָׁהּ בֶּן זוֹמָא, שֶׁנֶּאֱמַר: לְמַעַן תִּזְכֹּר אֶת יוֹם צֵאתְךָ מֵאֶרֶץ מִצְרַיִם כֹּל יְמֵי חַיֶּיךָ. יְמֵי חַיֶּיךָ הַיָּמִים; כֹּל יְמֵי חַיֶּיךָ הַלֵּילוֹת. וַחֲכָמִים אוֹמְרִים: יְמֵי חַיֶּיךָ הָעוֹלָם הַזֶּה; כֹּל יְמֵי חַיֶּיךָ לְהָבִיא לִימוֹת הַמָּשִׁיחַ.

---

*B'nai B'rak, flourishing today near Tel Aviv, may be the site of the ancient academy where these Rabbis met.

(The author of a fascinating biography of Akiba has suggested that these scholars were planning a revolt against the Romans – who had proscribed the study of Torah, under penalty of death.)

בָּרוּךְ הַמָּקוֹם, בָּרוּךְ הוּא.
בָּרוּךְ שֶׁנָּתַן תּוֹרָה לְעַמּוֹ יִשְׂרָאֵל,
בָּרוּךְ הוּא.

Praised be God; praised be He, praised be He who gave the Torah to His people Israel; praised be He.

Four times the Torah declares that parents should tell their children the story of Passover (Ex. 12:26; 13:8; 13:14; and Deut. 6:20). Thus the Sages infer that there are four types of children:

(1) The ḤAKHAM, variously translated as wise, clever, intelligent or mature;

(2) the RASHA, not wicked in the sense of an evildoer, but rebellious, scornful, stubborn and contemptuous, who does not inquire, and is irreverent and defiant;

(3) the TAM, the dull, simple, immature child;

(4) the SHE-ENO YO-DE-A LISH-OL, the child not yet capable of inquiring.

אַרְבָּעָה בָּנִים

THE FOUR CHILDREN

כְּנֶגֶד אַרְבָּעָה בָנִים דִּבְּרָה תוֹרָה:
אֶחָד חָכָם, וְאֶחָד רָשָׁע, וְאֶחָד תָּם,
וְאֶחָד שֶׁאֵינוֹ יוֹדֵעַ לִשְׁאוֹל.

The Torah speaks of four types of children: one who is wise, one who is rebellious, one who is simple, and one who does not know how to ask.

חָכָם מַה הוּא אוֹמֵר: מָה הָעֵדֹת
וְהַחֻקִּים וְהַמִּשְׁפָּטִים אֲשֶׁר צִוָּה יְיָ
אֱלֹהֵינוּ אֶתְכֶם: וְאַף אַתָּה אֱמָר לוֹ
כְּהִלְכוֹת הַפֶּסַח, אֵין מַפְטִירִין אַחַר
הַפֶּסַח אֲפִיקוֹמָן.

THE WISE CHILD asks, "What is the meaning of the laws, regulations and ordinances which the Lord our God has commanded you?" (Deut. 6:20) To such a child, explain all the laws of Passover even to the last detail, that nothing may be eaten and no entertainment or revelry is to take place after the AFIKOMAN.

THE REBELLIOUS CHILD asks: "What does this service mean to you?" (Ex. 12:26) By using the expression "to you," it is evident that our service has no significance for this child—who has separated from our people and denied God. Therefore, give a caustic answer and say: "It is because of what the Lord did for *me* when I came out of Egypt." (Ex. 13:8) "For me," not for such a one—who if in Egypt, would not have deserved to be liberated.

רָשָׁע מַה הוּא אוֹמֵר: מָה הָעֲבֹדָה הַזֹּאת לָכֶם? לָכֶם וְלֹא לוֹ. וּלְפִי שֶׁהוֹצִיא אֶת עַצְמוֹ מִן הַכְּלָל כָּפַר בָּעִקָּר. וְאַף אַתָּה הַקְהֵה אֶת שִׁנָּיו, וֶאֱמָר לוֹ: בַּעֲבוּר זֶה עָשָׂה יְיָ לִי בְּצֵאתִי מִמִּצְרָיִם. לִי וְלֹא לוֹ, אִלּוּ הָיָה שָׁם לֹא הָיָה נִגְאָל.

THE SIMPLE CHILD asks: "What does all this mean?" Say, "With a mighty hand, the Lord brought us out of Egypt, out of the house of bondage." (Ex. 13:14)

תָּם מַה הוּא אוֹמֵר: מַה זֹּאת? וְאָמַרְתָּ אֵלָיו: בְּחֹזֶק יָד הוֹצִיאָנוּ יְיָ מִמִּצְרַיִם, מִבֵּית עֲבָדִים.

וְשֶׁאֵינוֹ יוֹדֵעַ לִשְׁאוֹל – אַתְּ פְּתַח לוֹ, שֶׁנֶּאֱמַר: וְהִגַּדְתָּ לְבִנְךָ בַּיּוֹם הַהוּא לֵאמֹר: בַּעֲבוּר זֶה עָשָׂה יְיָ לִי בְּצֵאתִי מִמִּצְרָיִם.

AS FOR THE ONE WHO DOES NOT KNOW HOW TO ASK, you begin* by explaining, as we are told: "You shall tell your child on that day, 'I do this because of what the Lord did for me when I came out of Egypt.' " (Ex. 13:8)

יָכֹל מֵרֹאשׁ חֹדֶשׁ, תַּלְמוּד לוֹמַר: בַּיּוֹם הַהוּא. אִי בַּיּוֹם הַהוּא, יָכֹל מִבְּעוֹד יוֹם, תַּלְמוּד לוֹמַר: בַּעֲבוּר זֶה. בַּעֲבוּר זֶה לֹא אָמַרְתִּי אֶלָּא בְּשָׁעָה שֶׁיֵּשׁ מַצָּה וּמָרוֹר מֻנָּחִים לְפָנֶיךָ.

One might think that the Haggadah should be recited beginning with the first day of the month of Nisan. But the Bible says: "You shall tell your child *on that day*," (the fifteenth day of Nisan, the first day of Passover). One might infer *on that day* means in the daytime. But the verse continues: "I do this because of what the Lord did for me when I came out of Egypt," namely in the evening, when the matzah and bitter herbs are actually placed before you.

TWO KINDS OF SLAVERY

In accordance with the requirement that the reply to the Four Questions should "begin with the humiliation of a people and end with its glory," Samuel, head of the Nehardea Academy, preferred the opening passage to be "We were once slaves of Pharaoh in Egypt," whereas Rav, head of the Sura Academy, advocated the passage "Our ancestors were idol worshipers." (Pesaḥim 116a) Both of these passages were included; and they are interpreted to refer to two kinds of slavery from which the Israelites were emancipated: the first, that of physical bondage; the second, that of spiritual bondage. It is not enough to be free in body; one must be free also in spirit. Jews have frequently been threatened with both kinds of slavery—the slavery imposed from without, which sought to destroy the Jews physically, and the self-imposed slavery which destroyed spiritually those Jews who abandoned their faith and repudiated the traditions of their ancestors.

---

* The "You" in the sentence, "You begin . . ." is in the feminine form (*at*)—which was interpreted to mean that it is the mother who is to impart early instruction to the child.

מִתְּחִלָּה עוֹבְדֵי עֲבוֹדָה זָרָה הָיוּ אֲבוֹתֵינוּ, וְעַכְשָׁו קֵרְבָנוּ הַמָּקוֹם לַעֲבוֹדָתוֹ, שֶׁנֶּאֱמַר: וַיֹּאמֶר יְהוֹשֻׁעַ אֶל כָּל הָעָם, כֹּה אָמַר יְיָ אֱלֹהֵי יִשְׂרָאֵל, בְּעֵבֶר הַנָּהָר יָשְׁבוּ אֲבוֹתֵיכֶם מֵעוֹלָם, תֶּרַח אֲבִי אַבְרָהָם וַאֲבִי נָחוֹר; וַיַּעַבְדוּ אֱלֹהִים אֲחֵרִים. וָאֶקַּח אֶת אֲבִיכֶם אֶת אַבְרָהָם מֵעֵבֶר הַנָּהָר, וָאוֹלֵךְ אוֹתוֹ בְּכָל אֶרֶץ כְּנָעַן; וָאַרְבֶּה אֶת זַרְעוֹ, וָאֶתֶּן לוֹ אֶת יִצְחָק. וָאֶתֵּן לְיִצְחָק אֶת יַעֲקֹב וְאֶת עֵשָׂו; וָאֶתֵּן לְעֵשָׂו אֶת הַר שֵׂעִיר לָרֶשֶׁת אוֹתוֹ, וְיַעֲקֹב וּבָנָיו יָרְדוּ מִצְרָיִם.

In the beginning (before the days of Abraham), our ancestors were idol worshipers. God, however, called us to His service. For so we read in the Bible: "And Joshua said unto all the people, 'Thus said the Lord, God of Israel: In the days of old, your fathers, even Teraḥ, the father of Abraham and Naḥor, lived beyond the River Euphrates, and they worshiped idols. But I took your father, Abraham, from beyond the River Euphrates and I led him through the entire land of Canaan. I multiplied his offspring and gave him Isaac. To Isaac I gave Jacob and Esau. To Esau I gave Mount Seir as an inheritance; but Jacob and his sons went down into Egypt.'" (Josh. 24:2–4)

בָּרוּךְ שׁוֹמֵר הַבְטָחָתוֹ לְיִשְׂרָאֵל, בָּרוּךְ הוּא. שֶׁהַקָּדוֹשׁ בָּרוּךְ הוּא חִשַּׁב אֶת הַקֵּץ לַעֲשׂוֹת כְּמוֹ שֶׁאָמַר לְאַבְרָהָם אָבִינוּ בִּבְרִית בֵּין הַבְּתָרִים, שֶׁנֶּאֱמַר: וַיֹּאמֶר לְאַבְרָם, יָדֹעַ תֵּדַע כִּי גֵר יִהְיֶה זַרְעֲךָ בְּאֶרֶץ לֹא לָהֶם, וַעֲבָדוּם וְעִנּוּ אֹתָם, אַרְבַּע מֵאוֹת שָׁנָה. וְגַם אֶת הַגּוֹי אֲשֶׁר יַעֲבֹדוּ דָּן אָנֹכִי; וְאַחֲרֵי כֵן יֵצְאוּ בִּרְכֻשׁ גָּדוֹל.

Praised be God who keeps His promise to Israel; praised be He! For the Holy One, praised be He, determined the end of our bondage in order to fulfill His word, pledged in a solemn covenant to our father Abraham: "And God said to Abram, 'Know this for certain: your descendants shall be strangers in a land not their own, where they shall be enslaved and oppressed for four hundred years. But I will also bring judgment on the nation that held them in slavery; and in the end they shall go free with great substance.'" (Gen. 15:13, 14)

(Our Sages found meaning in every word and letter of the ancient text. For example, in the following prayer, they interpreted the first word, V'HI, thus: the VAV has the numerical value of six, and signifies the six divisions of the Mishnah; the HEH, the Five Books of Moses; the YOD, the Ten Commandments; and the ALEF, the One God.)

Faith to Face Our Adversaries

Cover the matzot and raise the cup of wine.

God's unfailing help has sustained our ancestors and us. For not only one enemy has risen up to destroy us, but in every generation do enemies rise up against us, seeking to destroy us; but the Holy One, praised be He, delivers us from their hands.

וְהִיא שֶׁעָמְדָה לַאֲבוֹתֵינוּ וְלָנוּ. שֶׁלֹּא אֶחָד בִּלְבָד, עָמַד עָלֵינוּ לְכַלּוֹתֵנוּ, אֶלָּא שֶׁבְּכָל דּוֹר וָדוֹר עוֹמְדִים עָלֵינוּ לְכַלּוֹתֵנוּ, וְהַקָּדוֹשׁ בָּרוּךְ הוּא מַצִּילֵנוּ מִיָּדָם.

V'hi she-amdah la-avotaynu v'lanu.
She-lo eḥad bil-vad amad alaynu le-ḥalotaynu,
Ela sheb-ḥol dor va-dor omdim alaynu le-ḥalotaynu,
Ve-ha-kadosh baruḥ hu matzilaynu mi-yadam.

The cup of wine is set down on the table. The matzot are uncovered.

Elaboration, Old and New...

(Additional passages may be introduced in this section, or continue at the middle of p. 20.)

We must be on guard against two kinds of enemies who would deprive us of our freedom: (1) the enemy without, easily recognized by his malicious words and evil deeds; and (2) the enemy within, posing as a friend and betraying us. Pharaoh was the enemy without and Laban, referred to in the passage which follows, symbolized the treacherous, false friend. By transposing the letters of the word ארמי ARAMI (Aramean) it becomes רמאי RAMAI, which means deceitful. In Jewish legend, Laban the Aramean (Syrian), not only attempted to annihilate Jacob and his descendants, but also incited others to destroy Israel.*

Let us consider what Laban the Aramean intended to do to Jacob. Whereas Pharaoh issued a decree against new-born males, Laban sought to annihilate Jacob and his entire family, for the Biblical verse may be read: "The Aramean wanted to destroy my father."

צֵא וּלְמַד, מַה בִּקֵּשׁ לָבָן הָאֲרַמִּי לַעֲשׂוֹת לְיַעֲקֹב אָבִינוּ. שֶׁפַּרְעֹה לֹא גָזַר אֶלָּא עַל הַזְּכָרִים, וְלָבָן בִּקֵּשׁ לַעֲקֹר אֶת הַכֹּל, שֶׁנֶּאֱמַר: אֲרַמִּי אֹבֵד אָבִי.

---

* It seems strange that Laban should be regarded as a greater menace to Israel than Pharaoh. A modern scholar maintains that this interpretation was given in the Third Century B.C.E., when Syria (Aram), typified by Laban, and Egypt, typified by Pharaoh, were rivals for the control of the Holy Land, then ruled by the Egyptian Ptolemies. Since the Haggadah is not favorable to Egypt, this Midrash was introduced as a gesture of good will towards the Egyptians, with whom the Jews of the region desired to live on friendly terms.

Supplementary Midrashim on the Biblical Narrative

The following are Midrashic interpretations of four Biblical verses (Deut. 26:5-8) which refer to the history of Israel and Egypt. These verses were recited annually by our ancestors during a ritual on Shavuot, when they brought their first fruits to the Temple at Jerusalem. Each Biblical word or phrase is analyzed and elaborated upon. The Haggadah is the only source of this exposition.

(1) אֲרַמִּי אֹבֵד אָבִי, וַיֵּרֶד מִצְרַיְמָה, וַיָּגָר שָׁם בִּמְתֵי מְעָט; וַיְהִי שָׁם לְגוֹי גָּדוֹל, עָצוּם וָרָב.

(1) "The Aramean wanted to destroy my father, but my father went down to Egypt and he sojourned there; (his household was) few in number, and there he became a nation, great, mighty and populous." (Deut. 26:5)

וַיֵּרֶד מִצְרַיְמָה: אָנוּס עַל פִּי הַדִּבּוּר.

"He went down to Egypt": compelled to do so by divine command.

וַיָּגָר שָׁם: מְלַמֵּד שֶׁלֹּא יָרַד יַעֲקֹב אָבִינוּ לְהִשְׁתַּקֵּעַ בְּמִצְרַיִם אֶלָּא לָגוּר שָׁם, שֶׁנֶּאֱמַר, וַיֹּאמְרוּ אֶל פַּרְעֹה, לָגוּר בָּאָרֶץ בָּאנוּ, כִּי אֵין מִרְעֶה לַצֹּאן אֲשֶׁר לַעֲבָדֶיךָ, כִּי כָבֵד הָרָעָב בְּאֶרֶץ כְּנָעַן; וְעַתָּה יֵשְׁבוּ נָא עֲבָדֶיךָ בְּאֶרֶץ גֹּשֶׁן.

"And sojourned there": from which we learn that Jacob did not intend to settle in Egypt, but only to dwell there temporarily, for the verse reads, "And the sons of Jacob said to Pharaoh, 'We have come to the land to dwell here temporarily, as there is no pasture for your servants' flocks, for the famine is severe in Canaan. Let then your servants dwell in the land of Goshen.'" (Gen. 47:4)

בִּמְתֵי מְעָט: כְּמוֹ שֶׁנֶּאֱמַר, בְּשִׁבְעִים נֶפֶשׁ יָרְדוּ אֲבֹתֶיךָ מִצְרָיְמָה; וְעַתָּה שָׂמְךָ יְיָ אֱלֹהֶיךָ כְּכוֹכְבֵי הַשָּׁמַיִם לָרֹב.

"Few in number": (as Moses said to the Children of Israel), "With only seventy souls your ancestors went down to Egypt; and now the Lord your God has made you as numerous as the stars of the heaven." (Deut. 10:22)

וַיְהִי שָׁם לְגוֹי: מְלַמֵּד שֶׁהָיוּ יִשְׂרָאֵל מְצֻיָּנִים שָׁם.

"And there he became a nation": indicating that even then the Israelites were identified as a distinct people.

גָּדוֹל, עָצוּם: כְּמוֹ שֶׁנֶּאֱמַר, וּבְנֵי יִשְׂרָאֵל פָּרוּ וַיִּשְׁרְצוּ, וַיִּרְבּוּ וַיַּעַצְמוּ בִּמְאֹד מְאֹד; וַתִּמָּלֵא הָאָרֶץ אֹתָם.

"Great and mighty": as we read, "And the Children of Israel were fruitful, and increased abundantly, and multiplied, and became great and mighty; and the land was filled with them." (Ex. 1:7)

וָרָב: כְּמוֹ שֶׁנֶּאֱמַר, רְבָבָה כְּצֶמַח הַשָּׂדֶה נְתַתִּיךְ; וַתִּרְבִּי וַתִּגְדְּלִי, וַתָּבֹאִי בַּעֲדִי עֲדָיִים; שָׁדַיִם נָכֹנוּ, וּשְׂעָרֵךְ צִמֵּחַ, וְאַתְּ עֵרֹם וְעֶרְיָה.

"And populous": as it is written in the Book of Ezekiel (16:7), "I have caused you to multiply as the buds of the field; you did multiply and grow in stature and beauty; your breasts were fashioned and your hair grew long; yet you were naked and bare."

(Though the Israelites had developed physically in Egypt, they were still spiritually immature because they had not yet received the Torah.)

(2) וַיָּרֵעוּ אֹתָנוּ הַמִּצְרִים וַיְעַנּוּנוּ, וַיִּתְּנוּ עָלֵינוּ עֲבֹדָה קָשָׁה.

(2) "And the Egyptians treated us harshly and oppressed us, and imposed hard labor upon us." (Deut. 26:6)

וַיָּרֵעוּ אֹתָנוּ הַמִּצְרִים: כְּמוֹ שֶׁנֶּאֱמַר, הָבָה נִתְחַכְּמָה לוֹ, פֶּן יִרְבֶּה, וְהָיָה כִּי תִקְרֶאנָה מִלְחָמָה, וְנוֹסַף גַּם הוּא עַל שֹׂנְאֵינוּ וְנִלְחַם בָּנוּ וְעָלָה מִן הָאָרֶץ.

"And the Egyptians treated us harshly": for as Pharaoh said, "Come let us outwit them lest they multiply and, in the event that we have war, they will join our enemies and fight against us, and escape from our land." (Ex. 1:10)

וַיְעַנּוּנוּ: כְּמוֹ שֶׁנֶּאֱמַר, וַיָּשִׂימוּ עָלָיו שָׂרֵי מִסִּים, לְמַעַן עַנֹּתוֹ בְּסִבְלֹתָם. וַיִּבֶן עָרֵי מִסְכְּנוֹת לְפַרְעֹה, אֶת פִּתֹם וְאֶת רַעַמְסֵס.

"And oppressed us": for the Bible tells us, "So the Egyptians appointed taskmasters over them to oppress them with heavy burdens; and the Israelites built for Pharaoh the treasure cities of Pithom and Raamses." (Ex. 1:11)

וַיִּתְּנוּ עָלֵינוּ עֲבֹדָה קָשָׁה: כְּמוֹ שֶׁנֶּאֱמַר, וַיַּעֲבִדוּ מִצְרַיִם אֶת בְּנֵי יִשְׂרָאֵל בְּפָרֶךְ.

"And they imposed hard labor upon us": as it is written, "The Egyptians imposed hard labor upon the Children of Israel." (Ex. 1:13)

(3) וַנִּצְעַק אֶל יְיָ אֱלֹהֵי אֲבֹתֵינוּ; וַיִּשְׁמַע יְיָ אֶת קֹלֵנוּ, וַיַּרְא אֶת עָנְיֵנוּ, וְאֶת עֲמָלֵנוּ וְאֶת לַחֲצֵנוּ.

(3) "And we cried unto the Lord, the God of our ancestors, and the Lord heard our cry, and saw our affliction, our travail and our oppression." (Deut. 26:7)

וַנִּצְעַק אֶל יְיָ אֱלֹהֵי אֲבוֹתֵינוּ: כְּמוֹ שֶׁנֶּאֱמַר, וַיְהִי בַיָּמִים הָרַבִּים הָהֵם, וַיָּמָת מֶלֶךְ מִצְרַיִם, וַיֵּאָנְחוּ בְנֵי יִשְׂרָאֵל מִן הָעֲבֹדָה וַיִּזְעָקוּ; וַתַּעַל שַׁוְעָתָם אֶל הָאֱלֹהִים מִן הָעֲבֹדָה.

"And we cried unto the Lord, the God of our ancestors": as the Bible tells us, "When many years had passed and the king of Egypt died, the Children of Israel moaned because of their bondage, and they cried; and from the midst of their slavery their cry came up to God." (Ex. 2:23)

וַיִּשְׁמַע יְיָ אֶת קֹלֵנוּ: כְּמוֹ שֶׁנֶּאֱמַר, וַיִּשְׁמַע אֱלֹהִים אֶת נַאֲקָתָם, וַיִּזְכֹּר אֱלֹהִים אֶת בְּרִיתוֹ אֶת אַבְרָהָם, אֶת יִצְחָק וְאֶת יַעֲקֹב.

"And the Lord heard our cry": as the verse relates, "God heard their groaning and God remembered His covenant with Abraham, with Isaac, and with Jacob." (Ex. 2:24)

וַיַּרְא אֶת עָנְיֵנוּ: זוֹ פְּרִישׁוּת דֶּרֶךְ אֶרֶץ, כְּמוֹ שֶׁנֶּאֱמַר, וַיַּרְא אֱלֹהִים אֶת בְּנֵי יִשְׂרָאֵל, וַיֵּדַע אֱלֹהִים.

"And He saw our affliction": this phrase refers to the enforced separation of husbands and wives. This is the interpretation of the verse, "And God saw the Children of Israel, and God knew their plight." (Ex. 2:25)

"And our travail": this recalls the drowning of the children, as it is written, "Every son that is born you shall cast into the Nile, but every daughter you may allow to live." (Ex. 1:22)

וְאֶת עֲמָלֵנוּ: אֵלּוּ הַבָּנִים, כְּמוֹ שֶׁנֶּאֱמַר, כָּל הַבֵּן הַיִּלּוֹד הַיְאֹרָה תַּשְׁלִיכֻהוּ, וְכָל הַבַּת תְּחַיּוּן.

"And our oppression": this refers to their persecution, of which the Bible says, "I have also seen the oppression wherewith the Egyptians oppressed them." (Ex. 3:9)

וְאֶת לַחֲצֵנוּ: זֶה הַדְּחַק, כְּמוֹ שֶׁנֶּאֱמַר, וְגַם רָאִיתִי אֶת הַלַּחַץ אֲשֶׁר מִצְרַיִם לֹחֲצִים אֹתָם.

(4) "And the Lord brought us out of Egypt with a mighty hand, with outstretched arm, in the midst of great awe, signs, and wonders." (Deut. 26:8)

(4) וַיּוֹצִאֵנוּ יְיָ מִמִּצְרַיִם, בְּיָד חֲזָקָה וּבִזְרֹעַ נְטוּיָה, וּבְמֹרָא גָּדֹל, וּבְאֹתוֹת וּבְמֹפְתִים.

"And the Lord brought us out of Egypt": not by any intermediary angel, seraph, or messenger, but by God Himself, in His glory, the Holy One, praised be He. For the Bible records, "I will pass through the land of Egypt on that night and I will smite all the first-born in the land of Egypt, both man and beast, and I will execute judgments against all the gods of Egypt. I am the Lord." (Ex. 12:12)

וַיּוֹצִאֵנוּ יְיָ מִמִּצְרַיִם: לֹא עַל יְדֵי מַלְאָךְ, וְלֹא עַל יְדֵי שָׂרָף, וְלֹא עַל יְדֵי שָׁלִיחַ, אֶלָּא הַקָּדוֹשׁ בָּרוּךְ הוּא בִּכְבוֹדוֹ וּבְעַצְמוֹ, שֶׁנֶּאֱמַר, וְעָבַרְתִּי בְאֶרֶץ מִצְרַיִם בַּלַּיְלָה הַזֶּה, וְהִכֵּיתִי כָל בְּכוֹר בְּאֶרֶץ מִצְרַיִם, מֵאָדָם וְעַד בְּהֵמָה; וּבְכָל אֱלֹהֵי מִצְרַיִם אֶעֱשֶׂה שְׁפָטִים, אֲנִי יְיָ.

"I will pass through the land of Egypt on that night": I, and not an angel; "I will smite all the first-born in the land of Egypt": I, and not a seraph. "And against all the gods of Egypt I will execute judgments": I, and not a messenger. "I am the Lord": I am He, there is no other.

וְעָבַרְתִּי בְאֶרֶץ מִצְרַיִם בַּלַּיְלָה הַזֶּה: אֲנִי וְלֹא מַלְאָךְ; וְהִכֵּיתִי כָל בְּכוֹר בְּאֶרֶץ מִצְרַיִם: אֲנִי וְלֹא שָׂרָף. וּבְכָל אֱלֹהֵי מִצְרַיִם אֶעֱשֶׂה שְׁפָטִים: אֲנִי וְלֹא הַשָּׁלִיחַ. אֲנִי יְיָ: אֲנִי הוּא וְלֹא אַחֵר.

"With a mighty hand": this refers to the cattle plague (even as Pharaoh was warned), "Behold the *hand* of the Lord will smite with a deadly pestilence your cattle in the field, your horses, donkeys, camels, herds and flocks." (Ex. 9:3)

בְּיָד חֲזָקָה: זוֹ הַדֶּבֶר, כְּמוֹ שֶׁנֶּאֱמַר, הִנֵּה יַד יְיָ הוֹיָה בְּמִקְנְךָ אֲשֶׁר בַּשָּׂדֶה, בַּסּוּסִים, בַּחֲמֹרִים, בַּגְּמַלִּים, בַּבָּקָר וּבַצֹּאן, דֶּבֶר כָּבֵד מְאֹד.

"And with outstretched arm": this suggests the sword of destruction as we read, "And the drawn sword in his hand, outstretched over Jerusalem." (1 Chron. 21:16)

וּבִזְרֹעַ נְטוּיָה: זוֹ הַחֶרֶב, כְּמוֹ שֶׁנֶּאֱמַר, וְחַרְבּוֹ שְׁלוּפָה בְּיָדוֹ, נְטוּיָה עַל יְרוּשָׁלָיִם.

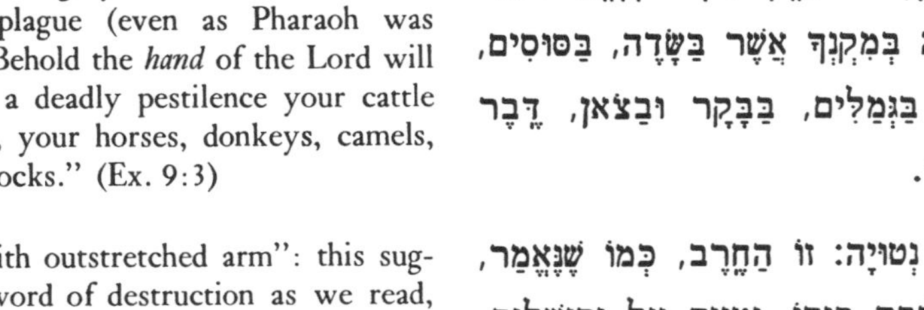

וּבְמֹרָא גָּדֹל: זוֹ גִּלּוּי שְׁכִינָה, כְּמוֹ שֶׁנֶּאֱמַר, אוֹ הֲנִסָּה אֱלֹהִים, לָבוֹא לָקַחַת לוֹ גוֹי מִקֶּרֶב גּוֹי, בְּמַסֹּת, בְּאֹתֹת וּבְמוֹפְתִים וּבְמִלְחָמָה, וּבְיָד חֲזָקָה וּבִזְרוֹעַ נְטוּיָה, וּבְמוֹרָאִים גְּדֹלִים, כְּכֹל אֲשֶׁר עָשָׂה לָכֶם יְיָ אֱלֹהֵיכֶם, בְּמִצְרַיִם לְעֵינֶיךָ?

"In the midst of great awe": this refers to the revelation of the Divine Presence. We understand this from the verse, "Has God ever sought to go and take for Himself a nation out of the midst of another nation, by trials, signs, wonders, war, by a mighty hand, outstretched arm, and by great awe, just as the Lord your God did for you, before your very eyes, in Egypt?" (Deut. 4:34)

וּבְאֹתוֹת: זֶה הַמַּטֶּה, כְּמוֹ שֶׁנֶּאֱמַר, וְאֶת הַמַּטֶּה הַזֶּה תִּקַּח בְּיָדֶךָ, אֲשֶׁר תַּעֲשֶׂה בּוֹ אֶת הָאֹתֹת.

"Signs": this alludes to the rod of Moses, as we are told, "Take this rod in your hand, and with it perform signs.' (Ex. 4:17)

וּבְמֹפְתִים: זֶה הַדָּם, כְּמוֹ שֶׁנֶּאֱמַר, וְנָתַתִּי מוֹפְתִים בַּשָּׁמַיִם וּבָאָרֶץ:

"Wonders": this refers to the miracle where the water of Egypt turned into blood as we see from the verse, "I will show wonders in the heavens and on the earth:

With a small spoon, spill from your cup some wine for each of the three miracles.

דָּם, וָאֵשׁ, וְתִמְרוֹת עָשָׁן.

Blood, fire, and pillars of smoke." (Joel 3:3)

דָּבָר אַחֵר: בְּיָד חֲזָקָה שְׁתַּיִם; וּבִזְרֹעַ נְטוּיָה שְׁתַּיִם; וּבְמֹרָא גָּדֹל שְׁתַּיִם; וּבְאֹתוֹת שְׁתַּיִם; וּבְמֹפְתִים שְׁתַּיִם.

Another interpretation (of Deut. 26:8) is: *strong hand*, indicates two plagues; *outstretched arm*, two plagues; *great awe*, two plagues; *signs* (since it is in the plural), two plagues; and *wonders* (in the plural), two plagues; thus making the ten plagues.

"LESS THAN FULL JOY"
(Thoughts Before Reciting the Ten Plagues)

As we read in the Haggadah about each of the plagues visited upon the Egyptians, we use a small spoon to remove some wine (onto our plate). The Psalmist says: "Wine makes glad the human heart." But how can we fully rejoice as we celebrate our freedom when we know that our redemption involved the suffering of the Egyptians?

We cannot be fully joyous when any human being, even an enemy, is afflicted. Hence, our Second "Cup of Joy" cannot be full; the symbol of gladness is diminished by the wine we spill to express sorrow for the Egyptians.

The Midrash relates that when the Egyptians were drowning in the Sea and the angels wanted to sing Halleluyah, God rebuked them: "How can you sing Halleluyah when My children are drowning?" (Talmud, Megillah 10b)*

In God's eyes all people are His children, and all nations His creation. "Have we not all one Father? Has not one God created us all?" (Mal. 2:10) "Are you not like the children of the Ethiopians unto Me, O Children of Israel?" says the Lord. (Amos 9:7)

* That is why only the short form of Hallel (Psalms of Praise), and not the full form of Hallel, is recited during the last six days of Passover.

This is one of numerous teachings which refute the old libel that Judaism is vindictive and does not emphasize love. In our Scriptures we find many examples of the Jewish emphasis on love. In the Five Books of Moses we are told: "Love thy neighbor as thyself." (Lev. 19:18) The Book of Proverbs cautions us: "Rejoice not when your enemy falls." (Prov. 24:17)

THE TEN PLAGUES

With a small spoon, remove a drop of wine from your cup into your plate, as each plague is mentioned.

These were the ten plagues which the Holy One, praised be He, brought upon the Egyptians in Egypt:

אֵלּוּ עֶשֶׂר מַכּוֹת שֶׁהֵבִיא הַקָּדוֹשׁ בָּרוּךְ הוּא עַל הַמִּצְרִים בְּמִצְרַיִם, וְאֵלּוּ הֵן:

דָּם, צְפַרְדֵּעַ, כִּנִּים, עָרוֹב, דֶּבֶר,
שְׁחִין, בָּרָד, אַרְבֶּה, חֹשֶׁךְ, מַכַּת בְּכוֹרוֹת.

Dam, Tz'fardea, Kinnim, Arov, Dever,
Sh'ḥin, Barad, Arbeh, Ḥoshekh, Makat b'khorot.

(1) Blood, (2) Frogs, (3) Vermin, (4) Wild Beasts, (5) Cattle Disease, (6) Boils, (7) Hail, (8) Locusts, (9) Darkness, (10) Smiting of the First-Born.

To facilitate remembering the order of the ten plagues as they occurred, Rabbi Judah put together the first Hebrew letter of each plague and formed three "words."

As each of the three "words" is mentioned, remove some wine from your cup.

Rabbi Judah used to refer to these plagues as follows:

רַבִּי יְהוּדָה הָיָה נוֹתֵן בָּהֶם סִמָּנִים:

D'TZaKH, ADaSH, B'AḤaB.

דְּצַ"ךְ, עֲדַ"שׁ, בְּאַחַ"ב.

(Ancient sources vary as to the nature and number of the plagues [see Psalm 78, Psalm 105, Book of Jubilees]. According to one scholar, these three phrases were intended to popularize the version recounted in Exodus, chapters 7-11.)

EVEN MORE MIRACLES: Some Ancient Elaborations

(In applying the tradition of "dwelling at length on the story of the Exodus," the Sages vied with one another in magnifying the number of miracles which occurred. In the following passages, the Sages interpreted various verses to indicate that there were as many as two hundred and fifty plagues! Thus they magnified the mercy and protection of God in sparing the Israelites.)

רַבִּי יוֹסֵי הַגְּלִילִי אוֹמֵר: מִנַּיִן אַתָּה אוֹמֵר שֶׁלָּקוּ הַמִּצְרִים בְּמִצְרַיִם עֶשֶׂר מַכּוֹת, וְעַל הַיָּם לָקוּ חֲמִשִּׁים מַכּוֹת? בְּמִצְרַיִם מַה הוּא אוֹמֵר? וַיֹּאמְרוּ הַחַרְטֻמִּים אֶל פַּרְעֹה, אֶצְבַּע אֱלֹהִים הִיא. וְעַל הַיָּם מַה הוּא אוֹמֵר? וַיַּרְא יִשְׂרָאֵל אֶת הַיָּד הַגְּדוֹלָה אֲשֶׁר עָשָׂה יְיָ בְּמִצְרַיִם, וַיִּירְאוּ הָעָם אֶת יְיָ; וַיַּאֲמִינוּ בַּייָ וּבְמֹשֶׁה עַבְדּוֹ. כַּמָּה לָקוּ בְּאֶצְבַּע? עֶשֶׂר מַכּוֹת. אֱמוֹר מֵעַתָּה: בְּמִצְרַיִם לָקוּ עֶשֶׂר מַכּוֹת, וְעַל הַיָּם לָקוּ חֲמִשִּׁים מַכּוֹת.

Rabbi Jose, the Galilean, asked how can one deduce that if the Egyptians were smitten with ten plagues in Egypt, they were smitten with fifty plagues at the Red Sea? Referring to the plagues in Egypt, the Bible says: "And the magicians said to Pharaoh, 'This is the *finger* of God.' " (Ex. 8:15) At the Red Sea, however, the Bible says: "And Israel saw the great *hand* which the Lord laid upon the Egyptians, and the people stood in awe of the Lord, and they believed in the Lord, and in His servant Moses." (Ex. 14:31) If, in Egypt, one finger of God caused ten plagues, then we may assume that at the Red Sea the whole hand of God brought fifty plagues.

רַבִּי אֱלִיעֶזֶר אוֹמֵר: מִנַּיִן שֶׁכָּל מַכָּה וּמַכָּה, שֶׁהֵבִיא הַקָּדוֹשׁ בָּרוּךְ הוּא עַל הַמִּצְרִים בְּמִצְרַיִם, הָיְתָה שֶׁל אַרְבַּע מַכּוֹת? שֶׁנֶּאֱמַר: יְשַׁלַּח בָּם חֲרוֹן אַפּוֹ, עֶבְרָה, וָזַעַם, וְצָרָה, מִשְׁלַחַת מַלְאֲכֵי רָעִים. עֶבְרָה אַחַת, וָזַעַם שְׁתַּיִם, וְצָרָה שָׁלֹשׁ, מִשְׁלַחַת מַלְאֲכֵי רָעִים אַרְבַּע. אֱמוֹר מֵעַתָּה: בְּמִצְרַיִם לָקוּ אַרְבָּעִים מַכּוֹת, וְעַל הַיָּם לָקוּ מָאתַיִם מַכּוֹת.

Rabbi Eliezer asked how can you show that every plague which God visited upon the Egyptians was fourfold? We read in Psalms: "He sent against the Egyptians His burning anger: wrath, indignation, trouble, and messengers of evil." (78:49) "Wrath" indicates one; "indignation," two; "trouble," three; "messengers of evil," four. Therefore, if each plague is fourfold, in Egypt they were smitten with forty plagues, and at the Red Sea with two hundred.

רַבִּי עֲקִיבָא אוֹמֵר: מִנַּיִן שֶׁכָּל מַכָּה וּמַכָּה, שֶׁהֵבִיא הַקָּדוֹשׁ בָּרוּךְ הוּא עַל הַמִּצְרִים בְּמִצְרַיִם, הָיְתָה שֶׁל חָמֵשׁ מַכּוֹת? שֶׁנֶּאֱמַר: יְשַׁלַּח בָּם חֲרוֹן אַפּוֹ, עֶבְרָה, וָזַעַם, וְצָרָה, מִשְׁלַחַת מַלְאֲכֵי רָעִים. חֲרוֹן אַפּוֹ אַחַת, עֶבְרָה שְׁתַּיִם, וָזַעַם שָׁלֹשׁ, וְצָרָה אַרְבַּע, מִשְׁלַחַת מַלְאֲכֵי רָעִים חָמֵשׁ. אֱמוֹר מֵעַתָּה: בְּמִצְרַיִם לָקוּ חֲמִשִּׁים מַכּוֹת, וְעַל הַיָּם לָקוּ חֲמִשִּׁים וּמָאתַיִם מַכּוֹת.

Rabbi Akiba went further, and asked how can one infer that every plague which God inflicted upon the Egyptians in Egypt was really fivefold? The same verse in Psalms may be interpreted as follows: "His burning anger" indicates one; "wrath," two; "indignation," three; "trouble," four; and "messengers of evil," five. Thus, if the Egyptians were stricken by the finger of God with fifty plagues, it follows that at the Red Sea they were stricken by the whole hand of God with two hundred and fifty plagues.

דַּיֵּנוּ

DAYYENU

DAYYENU is a rising crescendo of thanksgiving, beginning with gratitude for physical deliverance, and ending with gratitude for the spiritual blessings of the Sabbath and the Torah.

(Freedom, while essential, is not enough. The Exodus must lead to Sinai. Our Sages taught: "Consider as truly free only one who studies and lives by the Torah." Freedom under law is necessary for security and happiness.)

The *fifteen* "divine favors" enumerated in DAYYENU are referred to as MAALOT. They are said to correspond to the *fifteen* psalms which begin with the caption, "SHIR HAMAALOT" ("A Song of Ascent"). These psalms are said to have been sung by the Levites as they ascended the *fifteen* steps leading to the Sanctuary. *Fifteen* in Hebrew numerology is YOD HEH, which designates the name of God.

The word DAYYENU has been variously translated as: "it would have sufficed," "we should have been content," "for that alone we should have been grateful," and "we would have thought it enough." We shall leave the word DAYYENU untranslated.

Let us join in singing this delightful hymn of thanksgiving!

(For the abbreviated "singing version" of Dayyenu, see page 25.)

How thankful we should be to God For His many deeds of kindness to us!	כַּמָּה מַעֲלוֹת טוֹבוֹת לַמָּקוֹם עָלֵינוּ!
Had God freed us from the Egyptians, And not wrought judgment upon them, DAYYENU.	אִלּוּ הוֹצִיאָנוּ מִמִּצְרַיִם, וְלֹא עָשָׂה בָהֶם שְׁפָטִים, דַּיֵּנוּ.
Had He wrought judgment upon the Egyptians, And not destroyed their gods, DAYYENU.	אִלּוּ עָשָׂה בָהֶם שְׁפָטִים, וְלֹא עָשָׂה בֵאלֹהֵיהֶם, דַּיֵּנוּ.
Had He destroyed their gods, And not smitten their first-born, DAYYENU.	אִלּוּ עָשָׂה בֵאלֹהֵיהֶם, וְלֹא הָרַג אֶת בְּכוֹרֵיהֶם, דַּיֵּנוּ.
Had He smitten their first-born, And not given us their treasure, DAYYENU.	אִלּוּ הָרַג אֶת בְּכוֹרֵיהֶם, וְלֹא נָתַן לָנוּ אֶת מָמוֹנָם, דַּיֵּנוּ.

Had He given us their treasure,
And not divided the Red Sea for us,

DAYYENU.

אִלּוּ נָתַן לָנוּ אֶת מָמוֹנָם,
וְלֹא קָרַע לָנוּ אֶת הַיָּם,
דַּיֵּנוּ.

Had He divided the Red Sea for us,
And not let us pass through it dry-shod,

DAYYENU.

אִלּוּ קָרַע לָנוּ אֶת הַיָּם,
וְלֹא הֶעֱבִירָנוּ בְתוֹכוֹ בֶּחָרָבָה,
דַּיֵּנוּ.

Had He let us pass through it dry-shod,
And not drowned our oppressors in it,

DAYYENU.

אִלּוּ הֶעֱבִירָנוּ בְתוֹכוֹ בֶּחָרָבָה,
וְלֹא שִׁקַּע צָרֵינוּ בְּתוֹכוֹ,
דַּיֵּנוּ.

Had He drowned our oppressors in it,
And not sustained us in the wilderness for forty years,

DAYYENU.

אִלּוּ שִׁקַּע צָרֵינוּ בְּתוֹכוֹ,
וְלֹא סִפֵּק צָרְכֵּנוּ בַּמִּדְבָּר
אַרְבָּעִים שָׁנָה,
דַּיֵּנוּ.

Had He sustained us in the wilderness for forty years,
And not fed us with manna,

DAYYENU.

אִלּוּ סִפֵּק צָרְכֵּנוּ בַּמִּדְבָּר
אַרְבָּעִים שָׁנָה,
וְלֹא הֶאֱכִילָנוּ אֶת הַמָּן,
דַּיֵּנוּ.

Had He fed us with manna,
And not given us the Sabbath,

DAYYENU.

אִלּוּ הֶאֱכִילָנוּ אֶת הַמָּן,
וְלֹא נָתַן לָנוּ אֶת הַשַּׁבָּת,
דַּיֵּנוּ.

Had He given us the Sabbath,
And not brought us to Mount Sinai,

DAYYENU.

אִלּוּ נָתַן לָנוּ אֶת הַשַּׁבָּת,
וְלֹא קֵרְבָנוּ לִפְנֵי הַר סִינַי,
דַּיֵּנוּ.

Had He brought us to Mount Sinai,
And not given us the Torah,

DAYYENU.

אִלּוּ קֵרְבָנוּ לִפְנֵי הַר סִינַי,
וְלֹא נָתַן לָנוּ אֶת הַתּוֹרָה,
דַּיֵּנוּ.

Had He given us the Torah,
And not brought us into the Land of Israel,
DAYYENU.

אִלּוּ נָתַן לָנוּ אֶת הַתּוֹרָה,
וְלֹא הִכְנִיסָנוּ לְאֶרֶץ יִשְׂרָאֵל,
דַּיֵּנוּ.

Had He brought us into the Land of Israel,
And not built the Temple for us,
DAYYENU.

אִלּוּ הִכְנִיסָנוּ לְאֶרֶץ יִשְׂרָאֵל,
וְלֹא בָנָה לָנוּ אֶת בֵּית הַבְּחִירָה,
דַּיֵּנוּ.

How manifold are God's blessings in double and redoubled measure! He freed us from the Egyptians and brought judgment upon them; He destroyed their gods and smote their first-born; He gave us their treasure and divided the Red Sea for us; He led us through it dry-shod, and drowned our oppressors in it; He sustained us in the wilderness for forty years and fed us with manna; He gave us the Sabbath and brought us to Mount Sinai; He gave us the Torah and brought us into the Land of Israel; He built for us the Temple where we prayed for the atonement of our sins.

עַל אַחַת כַּמָּה וְכַמָּה, טוֹבָה כְפוּלָה וּמְכֻפֶּלֶת לַמָּקוֹם עָלֵינוּ: שֶׁהוֹצִיאָנוּ מִמִּצְרַיִם, וְעָשָׂה בָהֶם שְׁפָטִים, וְעָשָׂה בֵאלֹהֵיהֶם, וְהָרַג אֶת בְּכוֹרֵיהֶם, וְנָתַן לָנוּ אֶת מָמוֹנָם, וְקָרַע לָנוּ אֶת הַיָּם, וְהֶעֱבִירָנוּ בְתוֹכוֹ בֶּחָרָבָה, וְשִׁקַּע צָרֵינוּ בְּתוֹכוֹ, וְסִפֵּק צָרְכֵּנוּ בַּמִּדְבָּר אַרְבָּעִים שָׁנָה, וְהֶאֱכִילָנוּ אֶת הַמָּן, וְנָתַן לָנוּ אֶת הַשַּׁבָּת, וְקֵרְבָנוּ לִפְנֵי הַר סִינַי, וְנָתַן לָנוּ אֶת הַתּוֹרָה, וְהִכְנִיסָנוּ לְאֶרֶץ יִשְׂרָאֵל, וּבָנָה לָנוּ אֶת בֵּית הַבְּחִירָה לְכַפֵּר עַל כָּל עֲוֹנוֹתֵינוּ.

Dayyenu

Eelu hotzi, hotzi-anu,
hotzi-anu mi-mitz-ra-yim,
hotzi-anu mi-mitz-ra-yim, Da-yey-nu.

אִלּוּ הוֹצִיא, הוֹצִיאָנוּ,
הוֹצִיאָנוּ מִמִּצְרַיִם (2), דַּיֵּנוּ.

Eelu natan, natan lanu,
natan lanu et ha-shabbat,
natan lanu et ha-shabbat, Da-yey-nu.

אִלּוּ נָתַן, נָתַן לָנוּ,
נָתַן לָנוּ אֶת הַשַּׁבָּת (2), דַּיֵּנוּ.

Eelu natan, natan lanu,
natan lanu et ha-torah,
natan lanu et ha-torah, Da-yey-nu.

אִלּוּ נָתַן, נָתַן לָנוּ,
נָתַן לָנוּ אֶת הַתּוֹרָה (2), דַּיֵּנוּ.

Eelu hiḥni, hiḥni-sanu l'eretz yisrael . . .

אִלּוּ הִכְנִיסָנוּ לְאֶרֶץ יִשְׂרָאֵל, דַּיֵּנוּ.

The Duty to Explain

Rabbi Gamaliel (grandson of the great Sage Hillel) said: "One who has not explained the following symbols of the Seder has not fulfilled the Festival obligations:

רַבָּן גַּמְלִיאֵל הָיָה אוֹמֵר: כָּל שֶׁלֹּא אָמַר שְׁלֹשָׁה דְבָרִים אֵלּוּ בַּפֶּסַח לֹא יָצָא יְדֵי חוֹבָתוֹ, וְאֵלּוּ הֵן:

Pesaḥ, the Paschal Lamb; — פֶּסַח,

Matzah, the Unleavened Bread; — מַצָּה,

Maror, the Bitter Herb. — וּמָרוֹר.

Three Seder Symbols

The following explanations of PESAḤ, MATZAH, *and* MAROR *are taken from the* MISHNAH (Pesaḥim 10:5).

QUESTION:

What is the meaning of the PASCHAL LAMB which our ancestors used to eat at the time when the Temple was still in existence?

פֶּסַח, שֶׁהָיוּ אֲבוֹתֵינוּ אוֹכְלִים בִּזְמַן שֶׁבֵּית הַמִּקְדָּשׁ הָיָה קַיָּם, עַל שׁוּם מָה?

ANSWER:

Point to the shank bone of the lamb and answer:

The PASCHAL LAMB is to remind us that the Holy One, praised be He, passed over the houses of our ancestors in Egypt, as it is written in the Bible: "You shall say that it is the sacrifice of the Lord's passover, for He passed over the houses of the Children of Israel in Egypt when He smote the Egyptians, but spared our houses. The people bowed their heads and worshiped." (Ex. 12:27)

עַל שׁוּם שֶׁפָּסַח הַקָּדוֹשׁ בָּרוּךְ הוּא
עַל בָּתֵּי אֲבוֹתֵינוּ בְּמִצְרַיִם, שֶׁנֶּאֱמַר:
וַאֲמַרְתֶּם זֶבַח פֶּסַח הוּא לַיְיָ, אֲשֶׁר
פָּסַח עַל בָּתֵּי בְנֵי יִשְׂרָאֵל בְּמִצְרַיִם,
בְּנָגְפּוֹ אֶת מִצְרַיִם וְאֶת בָּתֵּינוּ הִצִּיל;
וַיִּקֹּד הָעָם וַיִּשְׁתַּחֲווּ.

Some scholars maintain that because the Egyptians worshiped the lamb, that animal was deliberately chosen to be sacrificed on Passover—thus emphasizing the Israelite rejection of animal worship.

In the days before the destruction of the Temple, each family's Seder observance included the sacrifice of a lamb, which was then roasted and eaten. Later, when animal sacrifices were abolished, other meat was substituted. (However, any meat served at the Seder was not to be "roasted on an open flame" because the lamb of the former Paschal Sacrifice had been prepared in this manner.)

What an impressive sight it must have been when, from all parts of the Land, families of pilgrims gathered in Jerusalem to observe Passover.

In our day too, the Seder is the family celebration, *par excellence,* bringing together families and friends—from near and far.

How significant it is that the first ordinance of the Jewish religion concerns a *family* festival, celebrating the birth of *freedom*! (See Exodus 12:13.)

May the continued observance of the Seder in our generation help to make of each Jewish home "a miniature sanctuary in which God's spirit shall dwell"—and in which reverence, love, and peace shall endure.

QUESTION:

What is the meaning of the MATZAH that we eat?

מַצָּה זוֹ, שֶׁאָנוּ אוֹכְלִים,
עַל שׁוּם מָה?

ANSWER:

Raise the Matzah *and answer:*

The MATZAH is to remind us that before the dough which our ancestors prepared for bread had time to ferment, the supreme King of kings, the Holy One, praised be He, revealed Himself to them and redeemed them. We read in the Bible: "They baked matzah of the unleavened dough which they had brought out of Egypt, for it had not leavened because they were thrust out of Egypt and could not linger, nor had they prepared any food for the journey." (Ex. 12:39)

עַל שׁוּם שֶׁלֹּא הִסְפִּיק בְּצֵקָם שֶׁל אֲבוֹתֵינוּ לְהַחֲמִיץ עַד שֶׁנִּגְלָה עֲלֵיהֶם מֶלֶךְ מַלְכֵי הַמְּלָכִים, הַקָּדוֹשׁ בָּרוּךְ הוּא, וּגְאָלָם, שֶׁנֶּאֱמַר: וַיֹּאפוּ אֶת הַבָּצֵק אֲשֶׁר הוֹצִיאוּ מִמִּצְרַיִם, עֻגֹת מַצּוֹת כִּי לֹא חָמֵץ; כִּי גֹרְשׁוּ מִמִּצְרַיִם, וְלֹא יָכְלוּ לְהִתְמַהְמֵהַּ, וְגַם צֵדָה לֹא עָשׂוּ לָהֶם.

Our Sages sought to link ethical teachings to the Biblical command (Ex. 12:17): "You shall observe the Feast of Matzot."

- By changing the vowels of the word MATZOT, they said, it becomes MITZVOT, yielding "You shall observe the MITZVOT" (Commandments). Worthy deeds and rituals are interwoven in Judaism!
- Just as we should not allow matzah to sour by delaying its baking, so we should not permit the opportunity to perform a mitzvah to "sour" by postponing its performance.
- Leaven is a symbol of evil and selfishness. Just as we search for, and remove, all leaven from our homes, so should we search our hearts—and rid ourselves of all that degrades and debases.
- Since the enslavement of the Israelites preceded their emancipation, one would expect the Haggadah's explanation of the MAROR, symbol of bondage, to *precede* the explanation of the MATZAH, which reminds us of freedom. Yet, the reverse is the case. Why? To suggest that many among the enslaved tend to accept their conditions of servitude passively. (They may not really understand freedom—or its privileges and responsibilities.) That is why the explanation of the matzah, symbol of liberation, is emphasized first. Only those who have experienced freedom can fully understand the evils of oppression. It is, therefore, the duty of all who have attained freedom to work unceasingly for the liberation of those who are still oppressed.

QUESTION:

What is the meaning of the BITTER HERBS which we eat?

מָרוֹר זֶה, שֶׁאָנוּ אוֹכְלִים, עַל שׁוּם מָה?

ANSWER:

Point to the Maror *and answer:*

The MAROR is to remind us that the Egyptians embittered the lives of our ancestors in Egypt, as the Bible explains: "They made their lives bitter with hard labor, with mortar and brick, and with every kind of work in the field. All the labor which the Egyptians forced upon them was harsh." (Ex. 1:14)

עַל שׁוּם שֶׁמֵּרְרוּ הַמִּצְרִים אֶת חַיֵּי אֲבוֹתֵינוּ בְּמִצְרַיִם, שֶׁנֶּאֱמַר: וַיְמָרְרוּ אֶת חַיֵּיהֶם בַּעֲבֹדָה קָשָׁה, בְּחֹמֶר וּבִלְבֵנִים, וּבְכָל עֲבֹדָה בַּשָּׂדֶה; אֵת כָּל עֲבֹדָתָם אֲשֶׁר עָבְדוּ בָהֶם בְּפָרֶךְ.

The following passage emphasizes our strong bond with Jewish history, its unity and continuity. In every age, Pharaohs have arisen to oppress our people. The hurt of any Jew anywhere became the hurt of all Jews everywhere. We have come to feel, therefore, that when our people were slaves in Egypt, it is as though we too were slaves; when they were redeemed, *we* were redeemed!

Today, even though we are free, we hear the cries of those of our brothers and sisters who are oppressed—and of all others who are enslaved. We know that our concern must not cease until *all* who groan under the yoke of tyranny are free.

In Every Generation

IN every generation each of us should feel as though he or she personally went forth from Egypt. That is what the Bible means when it says: "And you shall tell your child on that day, saying, 'It is because of what the Lord did for *me* when I went forth from Egypt.' " (Ex. 13:8) It was not only our ancestors whom the Holy One, praised be He, redeemed from slavery, but us also did He redeem together with them, as we read: "He brought *us* out from there so that He might bring us into the land, and give us this land which He promised to our ancestors." (Deut. 6:23)

בְּכָל דּוֹר וָדוֹר חַיָּב אָדָם לִרְאוֹת אֶת עַצְמוֹ כְּאִלּוּ הוּא יָצָא מִמִּצְרָיִם, שֶׁנֶּאֱמַר: וְהִגַּדְתָּ לְבִנְךָ בַּיּוֹם הַהוּא לֵאמֹר: בַּעֲבוּר זֶה עָשָׂה יְיָ לִי בְּצֵאתִי מִמִּצְרָיִם. לֹא אֶת אֲבוֹתֵינוּ בִּלְבָד גָּאַל הַקָּדוֹשׁ בָּרוּךְ הוּא, אֶלָּא אַף אוֹתָנוּ גָּאַל עִמָּהֶם, שֶׁנֶּאֱמַר: וְאוֹתָנוּ הוֹצִיא מִשָּׁם, לְמַעַן הָבִיא אֹתָנוּ, לָתֶת לָנוּ אֶת הָאָרֶץ אֲשֶׁר נִשְׁבַּע לַאֲבֹתֵינוּ.

Grateful Praise

In gratitude for the miracles which God has performed for our ancestors and for us from the days of old to this time, we raise our cups of wine and together say:

Therefore, we should thank and praise, laud and glorify, exalt and honor, extol and adore God who performed all these miracles for our ancestors and for us. He brought us from slavery to freedom, from sorrow to joy, from mourning to festivity, from darkness to great light, and from bondage to redemption. Let us, then, sing unto Him a new song: Halleluyah, praise the Lord!

לְפִיכָךְ אֲנַחְנוּ חַיָּבִים לְהוֹדוֹת,
לְהַלֵּל, לְשַׁבֵּחַ, לְפָאֵר, לְרוֹמֵם,
לְהַדֵּר, לְבָרֵךְ, לְעַלֵּה וּלְקַלֵּס לְמִי
שֶׁעָשָׂה לַאֲבוֹתֵינוּ וְלָנוּ אֶת כָּל הַנִּסִּים
הָאֵלּוּ. הוֹצִיאָנוּ מֵעַבְדוּת לְחֵרוּת,
מִיָּגוֹן לְשִׂמְחָה, מֵאֵבֶל לְיוֹם טוֹב,
וּמֵאֲפֵלָה לְאוֹר גָּדוֹל, וּמִשִּׁעְבּוּד
לִגְאֻלָּה. וְנֹאמַר לְפָנָיו שִׁירָה חֲדָשָׁה;
הַלְלוּיָהּ!

V'nomar l'fanav shira ḥada-sha, halleluyah.

The wine cups are set down.

הַלֵּל

HALLEL

The following psalms in the Hallel are the same as those the Levites chanted in the Temple when the Paschal sacrifices were offered. Note the expression, "servants of the Lord." Our Sages explain: "Heretofore you were servants of Pharaoh; now you are servants of the Lord. You are My servants, and servants cannot possess other servants." (Talmud, Meg. 14a)

GOD CARES FOR THE LOWLY

Psalm 113

Halleluyah!

O servants of the Lord,
Praise the name of the Lord.

Praised be the name of the Lord
From this time forth and forever.

From the rising of the sun unto its setting,
The Lord's name is to be praised.

הַלְלוּיָהּ!
הַלְלוּ, עַבְדֵי יְיָ,
הַלְלוּ אֶת שֵׁם יְיָ.

יְהִי שֵׁם יְיָ מְבֹרָךְ,
מֵעַתָּה וְעַד עוֹלָם.

מִמִּזְרַח שֶׁמֶשׁ עַד מְבוֹאוֹ,
מְהֻלָּל שֵׁם יְיָ.

The Lord is supreme above all nations;
His glory is above the heavens.

רָם עַל כָּל גּוֹיִם יְיָ,
עַל הַשָּׁמַיִם כְּבוֹדוֹ.

Who is like the Lord our God,
Enthroned so high,

מִי כַּייָ אֱלֹהֵינוּ,
הַמַּגְבִּיהִי לָשָׁבֶת.

Yet who looks down,
To consider both heaven and earth?

הַמַּשְׁפִּילִי לִרְאוֹת
בַּשָּׁמַיִם וּבָאָרֶץ?

He raises up the poor out of the dust,
And lifts up the needy from the pit,

מְקִימִי מֵעָפָר דָּל,
מֵאַשְׁפֹּת יָרִים אֶבְיוֹן.

To seat them together with princes,
Together with the princes of his people.

לְהוֹשִׁיבִי עִם נְדִיבִים,
עִם נְדִיבֵי עַמּוֹ.

He makes the childless wife
A happy mother of children.

Halleluyah!

מוֹשִׁיבִי עֲקֶרֶת הַבַּיִת,
אֵם הַבָּנִים שְׂמֵחָה;
הַלְלוּיָהּ!

WHEN ISRAEL WENT FORTH FROM EGYPT

Psalm 114

Be-tzayt yisrael mi-mitzra-yim, bayt ya-akov may-am lo-ayz.

When Israel went forth from Egypt,
The house of Jacob from a people strange of tongue,

בְּצֵאת יִשְׂרָאֵל מִמִּצְרָיִם,
בֵּית יַעֲקֹב מֵעַם לֹעֵז.

Judah became God's Sanctuary,
Israel, His own dominion.

הָיְתָה יְהוּדָה לְקָדְשׁוֹ,
יִשְׂרָאֵל מַמְשְׁלוֹתָיו.

The sea saw it, and fled;
The Jordan turned back in its course.

הַיָּם רָאָה וַיָּנֹס;
הַיַּרְדֵּן יִסֹּב לְאָחוֹר.

The mountains, affrighted, skipped like rams,
The hills, like young lambs.

הֶהָרִים רָקְדוּ כְאֵילִים,
גְּבָעוֹת כִּבְנֵי צֹאן.

What ails you, O sea, that you flee?
O Jordan, that you turn back in your course?

מַה לְּךָ הַיָּם כִּי תָנוּס?
הַיַּרְדֵּן, תִּסֹּב לְאָחוֹר?

הֶהָרִים, תִּרְקְדוּ כְאֵילִים;
גְּבָעוֹת, כִּבְנֵי צֹאן?

You mountains, that you skip like rams;
And you hills, like young lambs?

מִלִּפְנֵי אָדוֹן חוּלִי אָרֶץ,
מִלִּפְנֵי אֱלוֹהַּ יַעֲקֹב.

Tremble, O earth, at the presence of the Lord,
At the presence of the God of Jacob,

הַהֹפְכִי הַצּוּר אֲגַם מָיִם,
חַלָּמִישׁ לְמַעְיְנוֹ מָיִם.

Who turns the rock into a pool of water,
The flinty rock into a flowing fountain.

Rabbi Akiba is responsible for including in the following prayer the hope of a future redemption — the restoration of Zion.*

This cup is not full because we spilled off some of its content when we enumerated the plagues inflicted upon the Egyptians. By drinking from this partially filled cup, we express our sympathy for the Egyptians who lost their lives when Israel attained freedom.

Participants raise their second cup of wine.

Redemption: Past and Future

בָּרוּךְ אַתָּה, יְיָ אֱלֹהֵינוּ, מֶלֶךְ
הָעוֹלָם, אֲשֶׁר גְּאָלָנוּ וְגָאַל אֶת אֲבוֹתֵינוּ
מִמִּצְרַיִם, וְהִגִּיעָנוּ לַלַּיְלָה הַזֶּה,
לֶאֱכָל בּוֹ מַצָּה וּמָרוֹר. כֵּן, יְיָ אֱלֹהֵינוּ
וֵאלֹהֵי אֲבוֹתֵינוּ, יַגִּיעֵנוּ לְמוֹעֲדִים
וְלִרְגָלִים אֲחֵרִים, הַבָּאִים לִקְרָאתֵנוּ
לְשָׁלוֹם, שְׂמֵחִים בְּבִנְיַן עִירֶךָ, וְשָׂשִׂים
בַּעֲבוֹדָתֶךָ. וְנֹאכַל שָׁם מִן הַזְּבָחִים
וּמִן הַפְּסָחִים, אֲשֶׁר יַגִּיעַ דָּמָם עַל
קִיר מִזְבַּחֲךָ לְרָצוֹן, וְנוֹדֶה לְךָ שִׁיר
חָדָשׁ עַל גְּאֻלָּתֵנוּ וְעַל פְּדוּת נַפְשֵׁנוּ.
בָּרוּךְ אַתָּה, יְיָ, גָּאַל יִשְׂרָאֵל.

Praised be Thou, O Lord our God, King of the universe, who redeemed us, and redeemed our ancestors from Egypt, and enabled us to reach this night on which we eat MATZAH and MAROR. Even so, Lord our God and God of our ancestors, do Thou enable us to reach in peace other holy days and festivals when we may rejoice in the restoration of Zion, Thy city, and find delight in serving Thee. There we shall partake of the Paschal meal and bring Thee the offerings which shall be acceptable unto Thee. And there we shall sing unto Thee a new song of praise for our freedom and redemption. Praised be Thou, O Lord, Redeemer of Israel.

After reciting the following blessing, drink the second cup of wine while reclining.

בָּרוּךְ אַתָּה יְיָ אֱלֹהֵינוּ מֶלֶךְ הָעוֹלָם בּוֹרֵא פְּרִי הַגָּפֶן:

בָּרוּךְ אַתָּה, יְיָ אֱלֹהֵינוּ, מֶלֶךְ הָעוֹלָם, בּוֹרֵא פְּרִי הַגָּפֶן.

Baruḥ atta Adonai, eloheynu meleḥ ha-olam, boray p'ri ha-gafen.

**Praised be Thou, O Lord our God, King of the Universe,
Creator of the Fruit of the Vine.**

---

* Thus in this prayer the masculine form, SHIR ḤADASH (a new song), denotes the deliverance that will take place in the future, whereas the feminine form SHIRAH ḤADASHAH, in the introduction to the Hallel (page 29), refers to the redemption from Egypt which has already taken place.

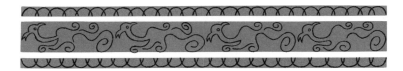

6. Raḥatz — Wash the Hands Before the Meal —

(Note the linking of hygiene & religion. Truly, "Cleanliness is next to Godliness.")

בָּרוּךְ אַתָּה, יְיָ אֱלֹהֵינוּ, מֶלֶךְ הָעוֹלָם, אֲשֶׁר קִדְּשָׁנוּ בְּמִצְוֹתָיו וְצִוָּנוּ
עַל נְטִילַת יָדָיִם.

Baruḥ atta Adonai, eloheynu meleḥ ha-olam,
asher kid-shanu b'mitzvo-tav, ve-tzivanu al ne-tilat yada-yim.

Praised Be Thou, O Lord our God, King of the Universe, Who hast Sanctified Us with Thy Commandments and Enjoined upon Us the Mitzvah of Washing the Hands.

7. Motzi — Say the Ha-Motzi —

8. Matzah — Recite the Blessing for the Matzah —

A piece of the uppermost matzah and a piece of the broken middle matzah are distributed to each participant. After salting the two pieces, recite the usual HA-MOTZI *and the special blessing for the matzah; then eat both pieces of matzah while reclining to the left.*

בָּרוּךְ אַתָּה, יְיָ אֱלֹהֵינוּ, מֶלֶךְ הָעוֹלָם, הַמּוֹצִיא לֶחֶם מִן הָאָרֶץ.

Baruḥ atta Adonai, eloheynu meleḥ ha-olam, ha-motzi leḥem min ha-aretz.

בָּרוּךְ אַתָּה, יְיָ אֱלֹהֵינוּ, מֶלֶךְ הָעוֹלָם, אֲשֶׁר קִדְּשָׁנוּ בְּמִצְוֹתָיו וְצִוָּנוּ
עַל אֲכִילַת מַצָּה.

Baruḥ atta Adonai, eloheynu meleḥ ha-olam,
asher kid-shanu b'mitzvo-tav, ve-tzivanu al aḥilat matza.

Praised be Thou, O Lord our God, King of the Universe, Who Bringest forth Sustenance from the Earth.

Praised be Thou, O Lord our God, King of the Universe, Who hast Sanctified Us with Thy Commandments and Enjoined upon Us the Mitzvah of Eating Unleavened Bread.

The matzah is salted as a reminder that all sacrifices brought into the Temple were salted before being burned on the altar.

We are obliged to eat matzah at the Seder only. We are not obliged to eat it at other times during the Passover festival; but we are to abstain from eating ḤAMETZ.

Matzah, the bread of poverty, is also vested with an ethical significance. Leaven is the symbol of YETZER HARA, the evil impulse. Matzah, the symbol of purity, represents freedom derived from obedience to the YETZER HATOV, the good inclination.

9. **Maror** — Eat the Bitter Herbs — מרור

The bitter herbs, of which we shall partake, are a reminder of the bitterness the Israelites experienced in Egypt. The ḤAROSET, into which the bitter herbs are dipped, symbolizes the mortar and bricks with which our ancestors were forced to construct cities and treasure-houses for Pharaoh.

Life is bitter-sweet. The sweet and pleasant taste of the ḤAROSET impresses upon us that, no matter how bitter and dark the present appears, we should hopefully look forward to better days. "Sweet are the uses of adversity." Since MAROR is a symbol of bondage, we do not recline while eating it.

A portion of the bitter herbs is dipped into the ḤAROSET *and eaten by each participant after reciting the following blessing:*

בָּרוּךְ אַתָּה, יְיָ אֱלֹהֵינוּ, מֶלֶךְ הָעוֹלָם, אֲשֶׁר קִדְּשָׁנוּ בְּמִצְוֹתָיו וְצִוָּנוּ
עַל אֲכִילַת מָרוֹר.

Baruḥ atta Adonai, eloheynu meleḥ ha-olam,
asher kid-shanu b'mitzvo-tav, ve-tzivanu al aḥilat maror.

Praised be Thou, O Lord our God, King of the Universe, Who hast Sanctified Us by Thy Commandments and Enjoined upon Us the Mitzvah of Eating the Bitter Herbs.

10. **Korekh** - Eat the Matzah and Maror Sandwich — כורך

(Called "Hillel's Sandwich")*

The bottom matzah is broken into small pieces. Each person receives two pieces between which are placed some of the bitter herbs.

To the Sage Hillel, eating MATZAH and MAROR together was not a trivial matter. To him, slavery and freedom were merged in one historical event. The bread of poverty became the bread of freedom and should be tasted together with the bitter MAROR, so that one should know the bitterness of slavery and the joy of freedom. In time of freedom, we must not forget the bitterness of slavery; in time of oppression, we must keep alive the hope of freedom. That is why Hillel's practice of eating MATZAH and MAROR together has such an important message for us today.

---

* The Sage Hillel, and not the Earl of Sandwich, the employer of Samuel Pepys, was the originator of the sandwich.

It was the Sage Hillel who, two thousand years ago, explained the essence of Judaism: "What is hateful to you, do not do to another. This is the whole Torah; the rest is the commentary thereof. Go and learn it." (Shab. 31a)

זֵכֶר לְמִקְדָּשׁ כְּהִלֵּל.

As a reminder of the Temple, we follow the practice of Hillel.

In unison

While the Temple was still in existence, Hillel would eat together in a sandwich some MATZAH and MAROR, to fulfill the Biblical command: "They shall eat it (the Paschal Lamb) together with unleavened bread and bitter herbs." (Num. 9:11)

כֵּן עָשָׂה הִלֵּל בִּזְמַן שֶׁבֵּית הַמִּקְדָּשׁ
הָיָה קַיָּם: הָיָה כּוֹרֵךְ (פֶּסַח) מַצָּה
וּמָרוֹר וְאוֹכֵל בְּיַחַד, לְקַיֵּם מַה
שֶּׁנֶּאֱמַר: עַל מַצּוֹת וּמְרֹרִים יֹאכְלֻהוּ.

All eat the sandwich.

11. Shulḥan Orekh — Enjoy the Festival Meal — שֻׁלְחָן עוֹרֵךְ

Now that we have completed the first part of the Haggadah, we are ready for the Passover meal—which will be followed by blessings, dramatic readings, psalms, and songs.

(When the Temple was in existence, roasted lamb was eaten at the Seder. Since the destruction of the Temple, lamb [and other foods roasted on an open flame] have been excluded from the Seder in most communities.)

Leader: As we savor the Seder dinner, we link physical delight and pleasure with our celebration of faith and freedom. Judaism calls upon us to serve God with all that we are and have.

In unison: As we enjoy our Festival meal, we pray that joy and contentment may soon be the lot of all God's children, in a world of peace and freedom.

Remove the Haggadot, etc., from the table and serve the meal.

In many homes, the meal begins with a hard-boiled egg dipped in salt water.*

---

*Three explanations are given for this custom. First, unlike most foods which become softer when boiled, the more an egg is boiled, the harder it becomes. This symbolizes the stubborn resistance of the Jews to those who sought to crush them. Secondly, the egg is regarded as the symbol of new life. Finally, since the roasted egg on the Seder plate is a reminder of the sacrifice that took place in the Temple of old, we eat the egg to remind us of the destruction of the Temple, and of our obligation to aid in the rebuilding of Zion.

(Interestingly, the first day of Passover always falls on the same day of the week as TISHAH B'AV, the ninth day of the month of AV, which commemorates the destruction of the first Temple by the Babylonians in 586 B.C.E., and of the second Temple by the Romans in 70 C.E.)

12. Tzafun — Eat the Afikoman — צָפוּן

Since the meal cannot be ritually completed without eating the AFIKOMAN, the Leader or Host now calls for the AFIKOMAN (the portion of the middle matzah that was hidden). The child who finds it receives a reward. The AFIKOMAN is our substitute for the Paschal Lamb, which in days of old, was the final food of the Seder feast. Each person is given a portion, which is eaten in a reclining position.

Fill the third cup of wine.

13. Barekh —
Recite the Birkat Hamazon (Blessing after the Meal) – בָּרֵךְ

BIRKAT HAMAZON is introduced with the singing of Psalm 126, which describes the joy of the exiles who returned from Babylonia to Zion twenty-five hundred years ago. Throughout the ages, this psalm brought hope to the Jews that Zion would be restored and provide a homeland for the homeless and oppressed of our people.

SHIR HA-MAALOT: Prelude to Birkat Hamazon

שִׁיר הַמַּעֲלוֹת.
בְּשׁוּב יְיָ אֶת שִׁיבַת צִיּוֹן
הָיִינוּ כְּחֹלְמִים.
אָז יִמָּלֵא שְׂחוֹק פִּינוּ,
וּלְשׁוֹנֵנוּ רִנָּה;
אָז יֹאמְרוּ בַגּוֹיִם,
הִגְדִּיל יְיָ לַעֲשׂוֹת עִם אֵלֶּה.
הִגְדִּיל יְיָ לַעֲשׂוֹת עִמָּנוּ,
הָיִינוּ שְׂמֵחִים.
שׁוּבָה יְיָ אֶת שְׁבִיתֵנוּ,
כַּאֲפִיקִים בַּנֶּגֶב.
הַזֹּרְעִים בְּדִמְעָה, בְּרִנָּה יִקְצֹרוּ.
הָלוֹךְ יֵלֵךְ וּבָכֹה נֹשֵׂא מֶשֶׁךְ הַזָּרַע;
בֹּא יָבֹא בְרִנָּה נֹשֵׂא אֲלֻמֹּתָיו.

Shir ha-ma-a-lot.
B'shuv Adonai et shivat tziyon
ha-yeenu k'ḥolmim.
Az yimalay s'ḥok peenu,
u-l'sho-naynu rina;
az yomru va-goyim,
higdil Adonai la-asot im ayleh.
Higdil Adonai la-asot imanu,
ha-yeenu s'mayḥim.
Shuva Adonai et sh'vitaynu,
ka-a-fikim ba-negev.
Ha-zoreem b'dima, b'rina yiktzoru.
Haloḥ yay-layḥ u-vaḥo,
nosay me-sheḥ ha-zara;
bo yavo v'rina nosay alumo-tav.

When the Lord brought the exiles back to Zion, we were as in a dream. Then was our mouth filled with laughter, and our tongue with joyous song. Then it was told among the nations: "The Lord has done great things for them." Yea, the Lord has done great things for us, and we are rejoiced. O Lord, bring back our exiles, like streams in the desert. They who sow in tears shall reap in joy. Though he weeps as he scatters his measure of seed, he shall return with joyous song as he carries home his sheaves. (Psalm 126)

BIRKAT HAMAZON (Grace after the Meal) *

(When ten or more are present, include the words in brackets.)

LEADER

Let us say the blessing for our food. רַבּוֹתַי, נְבָרֵךְ.

PARTICIPANTS, AND THEN LEADER

Praised be the name of the Lord from this time forth and forever.

יְהִי שֵׁם יְיָ מְבֹרָךְ מֵעַתָּה וְעַד עוֹלָם.

Y'hee shaym Adonai m'voraḥ may-atta v'ad olam.

LEADER

With the permission of those present, let us praise Him [our God] of whose bounty we have partaken.

בִּרְשׁוּת מָרָנָן וְרַבּוֹתַי נְבָרֵךְ [אֱלֹהֵינוּ] שֶׁאָכַלְנוּ מִשֶּׁלּוֹ.

PARTICIPANTS, THEN LEADER

Praised be He [our God] of whose bounty we have partaken and through whose goodness we live.

בָּרוּךְ [אֱלֹהֵינוּ] שֶׁאָכַלְנוּ מִשֶּׁלּוֹ וּבְטוּבוֹ חָיִינוּ.

Baruḥ [eloheynu] she-aḥalnu mi-shelo u-v'tuvo ḥa-yinu.

PARTICIPANTS AND LEADER

Praised be He and praised be His name. בָּרוּךְ הוּא וּבָרוּךְ שְׁמוֹ.

Baruḥ hu u-varuḥ sh'mo.

Baruḥ atta Adonai,
eloheynu meleḥ ha-olam,
ha-zan et ha-olam kulo b'tuvo,
b'ḥayn b'ḥesed u-v'raḥamim.
Hu notayn leḥem l'ḥol basar
kee l'olam ḥasdo.
U-v'tuvo ha-gadol
tamid lo ḥasar lanu,
v'al yeḥsar lanu
ma-zone l'olam va-ed,
ba-avur sh'mo ha-gadol.
Kee hu el zan u-m'farnays la-kol,
u-may-tiv la-kol, u-may-ḥin ma-zone
l'ḥol b'ri-yotav asher bara.
Baruḥ atta Adonai,
ha-zan et ha-kol.

בָּרוּךְ אַתָּה, יְיָ אֱלֹהֵינוּ, מֶלֶךְ הָעוֹלָם, הַזָּן אֶת הָעוֹלָם כֻּלּוֹ בְּטוּבוֹ, בְּחֵן בְּחֶסֶד וּבְרַחֲמִים. הוּא נוֹתֵן לֶחֶם לְכָל בָּשָׂר, כִּי לְעוֹלָם חַסְדּוֹ. וּבְטוּבוֹ הַגָּדוֹל תָּמִיד לֹא חָסַר לָנוּ, וְאַל יֶחְסַר לָנוּ מָזוֹן לְעוֹלָם וָעֶד בַּעֲבוּר שְׁמוֹ הַגָּדוֹל. כִּי הוּא אֵל זָן וּמְפַרְנֵס לַכֹּל, וּמֵטִיב לַכֹּל, וּמֵכִין מָזוֹן לְכָל בְּרִיּוֹתָיו אֲשֶׁר בָּרָא. בָּרוּךְ אַתָּה, יְיָ, הַזָּן אֶת הַכֹּל.

(Praised be God who by His grace sustains the world. May we never lack sustenance.)

BIRKAT HAMAZON *continues on pages 38 through 43.*
(If selected sections are excerpted, note transliterated passages for unison chanting.)

* *For a formally abbreviated version, see page 84.*

We thank Thee, O Lord our God, for the good, pleasant, and spacious land which Thou hast given as an inheritance to our ancestors, for having liberated us from the land of Egypt, and redeemed us from the house of bondage. We thank Thee for Thy covenant sealed in our flesh, for Thy Torah which Thou hast taught us, and for Thy laws which Thou hast made known to us. We also thank Thee for the gift of life which Thou, in Thy grace and lovingkindness, hast bestowed upon us, and for the sustenance with which Thou dost nourish and maintain us continually, in every season, every day, even every hour.

נוֹדֶה לְּךָ, יְיָ אֱלֹהֵינוּ, עַל שֶׁהִנְחַלְתָּ לַאֲבוֹתֵינוּ אֶרֶץ חֶמְדָּה טוֹבָה וּרְחָבָה; וְעַל שֶׁהוֹצֵאתָנוּ, יְיָ אֱלֹהֵינוּ, מֵאֶרֶץ מִצְרַיִם, וּפְדִיתָנוּ מִבֵּית עֲבָדִים; וְעַל בְּרִיתְךָ שֶׁחָתַמְתָּ בִּבְשָׂרֵנוּ; וְעַל תּוֹרָתְךָ שֶׁלִּמַּדְתָּנוּ; וְעַל חֻקֶּיךָ שֶׁהוֹדַעְתָּנוּ; וְעַל חַיִּים, חֵן וָחֶסֶד שֶׁחוֹנַנְתָּנוּ; וְעַל אֲכִילַת מָזוֹן שָׁאַתָּה זָן וּמְפַרְנֵס אוֹתָנוּ תָּמִיד, בְּכָל יוֹם וּבְכָל עֵת וּבְכָל שָׁעָה.

For all these blessings, O Lord our God, we give Thee thanks and we praise Thee. May Thy name be praised by every living being continually and forever, as we are told in the Torah: "When you have eaten and are satisfied, you shall praise the Lord your God for the good land which He has given you." (Deut. 8:10) Praised be Thou, O Lord, for the land and its produce.

וְעַל הַכֹּל, יְיָ אֱלֹהֵינוּ, אֲנַחְנוּ מוֹדִים לָךְ, וּמְבָרְכִים אוֹתָךְ; יִתְבָּרַךְ שִׁמְךָ בְּפִי כָּל חַי תָּמִיד לְעוֹלָם וָעֶד, כַּכָּתוּב: וְאָכַלְתָּ וְשָׂבָעְתָּ, וּבֵרַכְתָּ אֶת יְיָ אֱלֹהֶיךָ עַל הָאָרֶץ הַטֹּבָה אֲשֶׁר נָתַן לָךְ. בָּרוּךְ אַתָּה, יְיָ, עַל הָאָרֶץ וְעַל הַמָּזוֹן.

Ka-katuv, v'aḥalta v'savata u-vay-raḥta et Adonai elo-heḥa
al ha-aretz ha-tova asher natan laḥ.
Baruḥ atta Adonai, al ha-aretz v'al ha-mazon.

O Lord our God, remember in mercy, Israel Thy people, Jerusalem Thy city, Zion the abode of Thy glory, the royal house of David, Thine anointed, and the great and holy Temple called by Thy name. Our God and Father, tend and nourish us, sustain and maintain us, and speedily grant

רַחֵם, יְיָ אֱלֹהֵינוּ, עַל יִשְׂרָאֵל עַמֶּךָ, וְעַל יְרוּשָׁלַיִם עִירֶךָ, וְעַל צִיּוֹן מִשְׁכַּן כְּבוֹדֶךָ, וְעַל מַלְכוּת בֵּית דָּוִד מְשִׁיחֶךָ, וְעַל הַבַּיִת הַגָּדוֹל וְהַקָּדוֹשׁ שֶׁנִּקְרָא שִׁמְךָ עָלָיו. אֱלֹהֵינוּ, אָבִינוּ, רְעֵנוּ, זוּנֵנוּ, פַּרְנְסֵנוּ וְכַלְכְּלֵנוּ וְהַרְוִיחֵנוּ; וְהַרְוַח לָנוּ, יְיָ אֱלֹהֵינוּ,

מְהֵרָה מִכָּל צָרוֹתֵינוּ. וְנָא, אַל תַּצְרִיכֵנוּ, יְיָ אֱלֹהֵינוּ, לֹא לִידֵי מַתְּנַת בָּשָׂר וָדָם וְלֹא לִידֵי הַלְוָאָתָם, כִּי אִם לְיָדְךָ הַמְּלֵאָה הַפְּתוּחָה, הַקְּדוֹשָׁה וְהָרְחָבָה, שֶׁלֹּא נֵבוֹשׁ וְלֹא נִכָּלֵם לְעוֹלָם וָעֶד.

us surcease from all our sorrows. O Lord our God, let us not be dependent upon the alms of others or their favors, but rather let us look to Thy hand that is full, open and generous, so that we may never be humiliated or put to shame.

On Sabbath add:

רְצֵה וְהַחֲלִיצֵנוּ, יְיָ אֱלֹהֵינוּ בְּמִצְוֹתֶיךָ וּבְמִצְוַת יוֹם הַשְּׁבִיעִי הַשַּׁבָּת הַגָּדוֹל וְהַקָּדוֹשׁ הַזֶּה; כִּי יוֹם זֶה גָּדוֹל וְקָדוֹשׁ הוּא לְפָנֶיךָ, לִשְׁבָּת בּוֹ וְלָנוּחַ בּוֹ בְּאַהֲבָה כְּמִצְוַת רְצוֹנֶךָ. וּבִרְצוֹנְךָ הָנַח לָנוּ, יְיָ אֱלֹהֵינוּ, שֶׁלֹּא תְהֵא צָרָה, וְיָגוֹן וַאֲנָחָה, בְּיוֹם מְנוּחָתֵנוּ. וְהַרְאֵנוּ, יְיָ אֱלֹהֵינוּ, בְּנֶחָמַת צִיּוֹן עִירֶךָ, וּבְבִנְיַן יְרוּשָׁלַיִם עִיר קָדְשֶׁךָ, כִּי אַתָּה הוּא בַּעַל הַיְשׁוּעוֹת וּבַעַל הַנֶּחָמוֹת.

O Lord our God, strengthen us by Thy commandments, and especially by the commandment concerning the seventh day, this great and holy Sabbath. This day is great and holy before Thee, for in Thy love Thou hast decreed that we cease from all labor and rest thereon. O Lord our God, may it be Thy will to grant us such repose that no trouble, sorrow or anguish shall disturb our day of rest. May we behold Zion comforted, and Jerusalem, Thy holy city, rebuilt, for Thou art the Lord of redemption and of consolation.

אֱלֹהֵינוּ וֵאלֹהֵי אֲבוֹתֵינוּ, יַעֲלֶה וְיָבֹא, וְיַגִּיעַ וְיֵרָאֶה, וְיֵרָצֶה וְיִשָּׁמַע, וְיִפָּקֵד וְיִזָּכֵר זִכְרוֹנֵנוּ וּפִקְדוֹנֵנוּ, וְזִכְרוֹן אֲבוֹתֵינוּ, וְזִכְרוֹן מָשִׁיחַ בֶּן דָּוִד עַבְדֶּךָ, וְזִכְרוֹן יְרוּשָׁלַיִם עִיר קָדְשֶׁךָ, וְזִכְרוֹן כָּל עַמְּךָ בֵּית יִשְׂרָאֵל לְפָנֶיךָ, לִפְלֵיטָה וּלְטוֹבָה, לְחֵן וּלְחֶסֶד וּלְרַחֲמִים, לְחַיִּים וּלְשָׁלוֹם, בְּיוֹם חַג הַמַּצּוֹת הַזֶּה. זָכְרֵנוּ, יְיָ אֱלֹהֵינוּ, בּוֹ לְטוֹבָה וּפָקְדֵנוּ בוֹ לִבְרָכָה, וְהוֹשִׁיעֵנוּ בוֹ לְחַיִּים. וּבִדְבַר יְשׁוּעָה וְרַחֲמִים חוּס וְחָנֵּנוּ, וְרַחֵם עָלֵינוּ וְהוֹשִׁיעֵנוּ כִּי אֵלֶיךָ עֵינֵינוּ, כִּי אֵל מֶלֶךְ חַנּוּן וְרַחוּם אָתָּה.

Our God and God of our ancestors, on this Festival of Unleavened Bread, mayest Thou be mindful of us and our ancestors. Hasten the Messianic era; remember Jerusalem, Thy holy city, and all Thy people, the house of Israel, for deliverance, grace, lovingkindness, mercy, life and peace. Remember us this day, O Lord our God, to bless us with life and wellbeing. With Thy promise of deliverance and mercy, spare us and be gracious unto us, have compassion upon us and save us. We look to Thee, O our God, for Thou art a gracious and merciful King.

Rebuild Jerusalem, Thy holy city, speedily in our lifetime. Praised be Thou, O Lord, who in Thy mercy rebuildest Jerusalem. Amen.

וּבְנֵה יְרוּשָׁלַיִם עִיר הַקֹּדֶשׁ בִּמְהֵרָה בְיָמֵינוּ. בָּרוּךְ אַתָּה, יְיָ, בּוֹנֵה בְרַחֲמָיו יְרוּשָׁלָיִם, אָמֵן.

Uvnay yeru-shala-yim ir ha-kodesh bim-hayra ve-yamaynu.
Baruḥ atta Adonai, boneh ve-raḥamav yeru-shala-yim, amen.

Praised be Thou, O Lord our God, King of the universe. Thou art God, our Father, our Sovereign, our Mighty One, our Creator, our Redeemer, our Maker. O Holy One of Jacob, Thou art also our Holy One. O Shepherd of Israel, Thou art also our Shepherd. Thou art the good King who doest good to all. Thou who hast shown us kindness day by day and art good to us, mayest Thou continue Thy goodness to us. As Thou hast ever bestowed Thy bounties upon us, mayest Thou continue to bless us with Thy grace, lovingkindness, compassion and deliverance, prosperity, redemption and consolation, sustenance and mercy, a life of peace and all that is good. Mayest Thou never withhold Thy goodness from us.

בָּרוּךְ אַתָּה, יְיָ אֱלֹהֵינוּ, מֶלֶךְ הָעוֹלָם, הָאֵל, אָבִינוּ, מַלְכֵּנוּ, אַדִּירֵנוּ, בּוֹרְאֵנוּ, גּוֹאֲלֵנוּ, יוֹצְרֵנוּ, קְדוֹשֵׁנוּ, קְדוֹשׁ יַעֲקֹב, רוֹעֵנוּ, רוֹעֵה יִשְׂרָאֵל, הַמֶּלֶךְ הַטּוֹב וְהַמֵּטִיב לַכֹּל, שֶׁבְּכָל יוֹם וָיוֹם הוּא הֵטִיב, הוּא מֵטִיב, הוּא יֵיטִיב לָנוּ. הוּא גְמָלָנוּ, הוּא גוֹמְלֵנוּ, הוּא יִגְמְלֵנוּ לָעַד, לְחֵן וּלְחֶסֶד וּלְרַחֲמִים וּלְרֶוַח, הַצָּלָה וְהַצְלָחָה, בְּרָכָה וִישׁוּעָה, נֶחָמָה פַּרְנָסָה וְכַלְכָּלָה, וְרַחֲמִים וְחַיִּים וְשָׁלוֹם וְכָל טוֹב, וּמִכָּל טוּב לְעוֹלָם אַל יְחַסְּרֵנוּ.

May the Merciful One reign over us for ever and ever.

הָרַחֲמָן, הוּא יִמְלוֹךְ עָלֵינוּ לְעוֹלָם וָעֶד.

May the Merciful One be extolled in heaven and on earth.

הָרַחֲמָן, הוּא יִתְבָּרַךְ בַּשָּׁמַיִם וּבָאָרֶץ.

May the Merciful One be praised in all generations; may He be glorified through us to all eternity; may He be honored among us forever.

הָרַחֲמָן, הוּא יִשְׁתַּבַּח לְדוֹר דּוֹרִים, וְיִתְפָּאַר בָּנוּ לָעַד וּלְנֵצַח נְצָחִים, וְיִתְהַדַּר בָּנוּ לָעַד וּלְעוֹלְמֵי עוֹלָמִים.

May the Merciful One grant us an honorable livelihood.

הָרַחֲמָן, הוּא יְפַרְנְסֵנוּ בְּכָבוֹד.

May the Merciful One end our oppression and lead the homeless of our people in dignity into our ancient homeland.

הָרַחֲמָן, הוּא יִשְׁבּוֹר עֻלֵּנוּ מֵעַל צַוָּארֵנוּ, וְהוּא יוֹלִיכֵנוּ קוֹמְמִיּוּת לְאַרְצֵנוּ.

May the Merciful One grant abundant blessings upon this household and upon all who have eaten at this table [these tables].

הָרַחֲמָן, הוּא יִשְׁלַח בְּרָכָה מְרֻבָּה בַּבַּיִת הַזֶּה, וְעַל שֻׁלְחָן זֶה שֶׁאָכַלְנוּ עָלָיו.

May the Merciful One send us Elijah, the Prophet, be he remembered for his goodness; and may he announce to us good tidings of salvation and comfort.

הָרַחֲמָן, הוּא יִשְׁלַח לָנוּ אֶת אֵלִיָּהוּ הַנָּבִיא, זָכוּר לַטּוֹב, וִיבַשֶּׂר לָנוּ בְּשׂוֹרוֹת טוֹבוֹת, יְשׁוּעוֹת וְנֶחָמוֹת.

For Parents

May the Merciful One bless my revered father and teacher, and my esteemed mother and teacher, the heads of this household, them and all that is theirs.

הָרַחֲמָן, הוּא יְבָרֵךְ אֶת אָבִי מוֹרִי בַּעַל הַבַּיִת הַזֶּה וְאֶת אִמִּי מוֹרָתִי בַּעֲלַת הַבַּיִת הַזֶּה, אוֹתָם וְאֶת בֵּיתָם וְאֶת זַרְעָם וְאֶת כָּל אֲשֶׁר לָהֶם.

For the host

May the Merciful One bless our honored host and hostess, and all their dear ones.

הָרַחֲמָן, הוּא יְבָרֵךְ אֶת בַּעַל הַבַּיִת וְאֶת אִשְׁתּוֹ בַּעֲלַת הַבַּיִת הַזֶּה, אוֹתָם וְאֶת בֵּיתָם וְאֶת זַרְעָם וְאֶת כָּל אֲשֶׁר לָהֶם.

For spouse and children

May the Merciful One bless me and [my wife,] [my husband,] [my offspring,] and all that is mine.

הָרַחֲמָן, הוּא יְבָרֵךְ אוֹתִי [וְאֶת אִשְׁתִּי] [וְאֶת בַּעֲלִי] [וְאֶת זַרְעִי] וְאֶת כָּל אֲשֶׁר לִי.

For all those present

May the Merciful One bless all who are gathered at this table [these tables], them, their families, and all that is theirs.

הָרַחֲמָן, הוּא יְבָרֵךְ אֶת כָּל הַמְּסֻבִּין כָּאן, אוֹתָם וְאֶת זַרְעָם וְאֶת כָּל אֲשֶׁר לָהֶם.

May the Merciful One bless us and all who are dear to us, even as our fathers, Abraham, Isaac and Jacob were blessed, each with his own comprehensive blessing;* so, likewise, may He bless all of us together with a perfect blessing, and let us say, Amen.

הָרַחֲמָן, הוּא יְבָרֵךְ אוֹתָנוּ וְאֶת זַרְעֵנוּ וְאֶת כָּל אֲשֶׁר לָנוּ, כְּמוֹ שֶׁנִּתְבָּרְכוּ אֲבוֹתֵינוּ אַבְרָהָם יִצְחָק וְיַעֲקֹב בַּכֹּל, מִכֹּל, כֹּל, כֵּן יְבָרֵךְ אוֹתָנוּ כֻּלָּנוּ יַחַד בִּבְרָכָה שְׁלֵמָה, וְנֹאמַר אָמֵן.

May our merit and the merit of our ancestors secure for all of us enduring peace. May we receive a blessing from the Lord, and mercy from the God of our salvation. May we find grace and favor in the sight of God and humanity.

בַּמָּרוֹם יְלַמְּדוּ עֲלֵיהֶם וְעָלֵינוּ זְכוּת, שֶׁתְּהֵא לְמִשְׁמֶרֶת שָׁלוֹם. וְנִשָּׂא בְרָכָה מֵאֵת יְיָ, וּצְדָקָה מֵאֱלֹהֵי יִשְׁעֵנוּ, וְנִמְצָא חֵן וְשֵׂכֶל טוֹב בְּעֵינֵי אֱלֹהִים וְאָדָם.

On Shabbat: May the Merciful One find us worthy of the unending Sabbath and the serenity of the world to come.

On Shabbat הָרַחֲמָן, הוּא יַנְחִילֵנוּ יוֹם שֶׁכֻּלּוֹ שַׁבָּת וּמְנוּחָה לְחַיֵּי הָעוֹלָמִים.

May the Merciful One find us worthy of the time when complete felicity shall prevail.

הָרַחֲמָן, הוּא יַנְחִילֵנוּ יוֹם שֶׁכֻּלּוֹ טוֹב.

May the Merciful One bless the State of Israel and shield it from all peril.

הָרַחֲמָן, הוּא יְבָרֵךְ אֶת מְדִינַת יִשְׂרָאֵל וְיָגֵן עָלֶיהָ.

May the Merciful One find us worthy of the Messianic era and of the life to come.

הָרַחֲמָן, הוּא יְזַכֵּנוּ לִימוֹת הַמָּשִׁיחַ וּלְחַיֵּי הָעוֹלָם הַבָּא.

"He is a tower of deliverance to His (chosen) king, and shows kindness to His anointed one, to David and his descendants forever." (2 Sam. 22:51)

מִגְדּוֹל יְשׁוּעוֹת מַלְכּוֹ וְעֹשֶׂה חֶסֶד לִמְשִׁיחוֹ, לְדָוִד וּלְזַרְעוֹ עַד עוֹלָם.

May the Maker of peace in the heavenly spheres, grant peace to us, and to all Israel, and let us say, Amen.

עֹשֶׂה שָׁלוֹם בִּמְרוֹמָיו, הוּא יַעֲשֶׂה שָׁלוֹם עָלֵינוּ וְעַל כָּל יִשְׂרָאֵל, וְאִמְרוּ אָמֵן.

Migdol y'shuot malko v'oseh ḥesed li-m'sheeḥo, l'david u-l'zaro ad olam.

Oseh shalom bi-m'romav, hu ya-a-seh shalom alaynu v'al kol yisrael, v'imru amen.

* Gen. 24:1; 27:33; 33:11

Revere the Lord, you who are His holy ones; for those who revere Him suffer no want. Those who deny Him may lack food and suffer hunger, but they who seek the Lord shall not lack anything that is good. Give thanks unto the Lord for He is good; for His mercy endures forever. He opens His hand and satisfies every living thing with favor. Blessed is the man who trusts in the Lord; the Lord will be his protection. [Once I was young, now I am old; yet I have not seen the righteous forsaken or his offspring begging for bread.] The Lord will give strength to His people; the Lord will bless His people with peace.

(Ps. 34:10; 118:1; 145:16; Jer. 17:7; Ps. 37:25; 29:11.)

יִרְאוּ אֶת יְיָ קְדֹשָׁיו, כִּי אֵין מַחְסוֹר לִירֵאָיו. כְּפִירִים רָשׁוּ וְרָעֵבוּ, וְדֹרְשֵׁי יְיָ לֹא יַחְסְרוּ כָל טוֹב. הוֹדוּ לַיְיָ כִּי טוֹב, כִּי לְעוֹלָם חַסְדּוֹ. פּוֹתֵחַ אֶת יָדֶךָ, וּמַשְׂבִּיעַ לְכָל חַי רָצוֹן.

בָּרוּךְ הַגֶּבֶר אֲשֶׁר יִבְטַח בַּייָ, וְהָיָה יְיָ מִבְטַחוֹ.

[נַעַר הָיִיתִי גַּם זָקַנְתִּי, וְלֹא רָאִיתִי צַדִּיק נֶעֱזָב, וְזַרְעוֹ מְבַקֶּשׁ לָחֶם.]

יְיָ עֹז לְעַמּוֹ יִתֵּן; יְיָ יְבָרֵךְ אֶת עַמּוֹ בַשָּׁלוֹם.

After reciting the following blessing, drink the third cup of wine while reclining.

בָּרוּךְ אַתָּה יְיָ אֱלֹהֵינוּ מֶלֶךְ הָעוֹלָם בּוֹרֵא פְּרִי הַגָּפֶן:

בָּרוּךְ אַתָּה, יְיָ אֱלֹהֵינוּ, מֶלֶךְ הָעוֹלָם, בּוֹרֵא פְּרִי הַגָּפֶן.

Baruḥ atta Adonai, eloheynu meleḥ ha-olam, boray p'ri ha-gafen.

Praised be Thou, O Lord our God, King of the Universe, Creator of the Fruit of the Vine.

The fourth cup of wine is filled.
The special Cup of Elijah is also filled.

IN THE SPIRIT OF ELIJAH *

The Haggadah opens with the words: "Let all who are hungry come and eat." Among the awaited guests is the prophet Elijah who, according to tradition, never died, but was carried up to heaven.

The life of no other character in Jewish history is so surrounded with a halo of mystery and wonder as is that of Elijah. In Jewish legend, the ubiquitous Elijah is the champion of the oppressed. He brings hope, cheer, and relief to the downtrodden; and he performs miracles of rescue and deliverance.

It is Elijah, we are told, who can explain all difficult passages in the Bible and Talmud, and who will settle all future controversies. The prophet Malachi says of him: "He will turn the hearts of parents to their children, and the hearts of children to their parents." Elijah is the harbinger of good tidings of joy and peace.

Over the generations, the name of the wondrous Elijah became associated with the long-awaited "coming of the Messiah," whose advent he was expected to announce.

---

* According to a well-known legend, Elijah appears at every Seder and sips some wine from the cup reserved for him. Indeed, if the children are attentive and watchful, they may notice that, after the door is closed, there is a little less wine in Elijah's cup!

The door is opened. Let us rise, in the hope that Elijah will enter. With the salutation reserved for distinguished guests, let us say:

בָּרוּךְ הַבָּא

BARUḤ HA-BA — BLESSED BE HE WHO COMES!

As we sing the Song of Elijah, we pray that we may soon see fulfilled our hope for a world of freedom and peace for all.

Elijah, the Prophet; Elijah, the Tishbite; Elijah, the Gileadite; may he soon come and bring the Messiah.

אֵלִיָּהוּ הַנָּבִיא, אֵלִיָּהוּ הַתִּשְׁבִּי,
אֵלִיָּהוּ, אֵלִיָּהוּ, אֵלִיָּהוּ הַגִּלְעָדִי,
בִּמְהֵרָה יָבֹא אֵלֵינוּ עִם מָשִׁיחַ בֶּן דָּוִד.

Eliyahu ha-navi, eliyahu ha-tishbi, eliyahu, eliyahu, eliyahu ha-giladi, Bim-hay-ra [v'ya-maynu], yavo ay-laynu, in ma-shiaḥ ben david.

Participants are seated.

Alas, we now remember the thousands of Jews throughout our history for whom there was no deliverance. For centuries, our people were cruelly persecuted because they were determined to maintain their religious beliefs, traditions and ideals.*

The Jews did not retaliate against the inhumanities inflicted upon them. At the Seder, however, they vented their hurt and indignation by reciting the following Biblical verses:

"Pour out Thy wrath upon the heathen nations that do not acknowledge Thee and upon the kingdoms that do not call upon Thy name; for they have devoured Jacob and laid waste his dwelling place." (Ps. 79:6, 7)

שְׁפֹךְ חֲמָתְךָ אֶל הַגּוֹיִם אֲשֶׁר לֹא יְדָעוּךָ, וְעַל מַמְלָכוֹת אֲשֶׁר בְּשִׁמְךָ לֹא קָרָאוּ. כִּי אָכַל אֶת יַעֲקֹב, וְאֶת נָוֵהוּ הֵשַׁמּוּ.

"Pour out upon them Thine indignation, and let Thy fury overtake them." (Ps. 69:25)

שְׁפָךְ עֲלֵיהֶם זַעְמֶךָ, וַחֲרוֹן אַפְּךָ יַשִּׂיגֵם.

"Pursue them in anger and destroy them from under the heavens of the Lord." (Lam. 3:66)

תִּרְדֹּף בְּאַף וְתַשְׁמִידֵם מִתַּחַת שְׁמֵי יְיָ.

The door is closed.

---

* "Freedom of religion" is a comparatively new concept in the history of civilization; and religious strife still afflicts our world. Over the centuries, Jews were maliciously accused of using the blood of Christians in the baking of unleavened bread.** Despite assurances by some spiritual and temporal rulers that these charges were false and without foundation, bigots used the accusation as a pretext for looting Jewish homes and shops and brutally massacring men, women, and children. The notorious trial of Mendel Beilis, against whom a "blood accusation" made in Russia in 1911, was not the last such incident. Amazingly, even in post-Holocaust Europe, the "blood libel" was revived by anti-Semites.

** Early Christians were themselves accused by the pagans of using human blood in *their* ritual; and, in the Middle Ages, heretical Christians were similarly accused by other Christians!

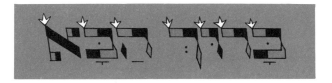

To Recall, to Reflect, to Resolve...

At this point in our Seder, we introduce material relating to events and experiences of recent Jewish history and to the concerns of contemporary life.

The selections on these two pages (45–46) may be recited either as one continuous reading or *as three distinct passages—each setting the tone for the introduction of optional, supplementary texts selected for this year's Seder.*

WE REMEMBER THE HOLOCAUST

Let us now pause to recall the bitter catastrophe which recently befell our people in Europe.

Responsive Reading

When in the past our brothers were massacred in ruthless pogroms, the poet Bialik, in his "City of Slaughter," cried out against the bloody savagery.

Today we mourn, not for one "city of slaughter" but for *many* such cities, where six million of our people have been brutally destroyed.

The cruelties of Pharaoh, Haman, Nebuchadnezzar, and Titus, cannot be compared to the diabolical devices fashioned by modern tyrants in their design to exterminate a whole people.

No generation has known a catastrophe so vast and tragic!

The blood of the innocent, who perished in the gas-chambers of Auschwitz, Bergen-Belsen, Buchenwald, Dachau, Majdanek, Treblinka, and Theresienstadt, cries out to God and to man.

How can we ever forget the burning of synagogues and houses of study, the destruction of the holy books and scrolls of the Torah, the sadistic torment and murder of our scholars, sages, and teachers?

They tortured the flesh of our brothers and sisters;
but they could not crush their spirit, their faith, or their love of Torah.

The parchment of the Torah was burnt; but the letters were indestructible.

In the Warsaw Ghetto, Jews valiantly defied the overwhelming forces of the inhuman tyrant. These martyrs lifted up their voices in a hymn reaffirming their faith in the coming of the Messiah, when justice and peace shall finally be established.

"I believe with a perfect faith in the coming of the Messiah;
and though he tarry, nonetheless do I believe he will come!"

Anee ma-a-min be-emuna sh'lay-ma be-veeat ha-ma-shiaḥ;
V'af al pee sheh-yitmah-may-ah, im kol zeh anee ma-a-min.

אֲנִי מַאֲמִין בֶּאֱמוּנָה שְׁלֵמָה בְּבִיאַת הַמָּשִׁיחַ;
וְאַף עַל פִּי שֶׁיִּתְמַהְמֵהַּ, עִם כָּל זֶה [אֲחַכֶּה לוֹ בְּכָל יוֹם שֶׁיָּבֹא] אֲנִי מַאֲמִין...

MEMORIAL, TRIBUTE, AND HOPE

Let us pray: O Lord, remember Thy martyred children; remember all who have given their lives for KIDDUSH HASHEM, the sanctification of Thy name.

> Grant their souls the peace reserved for all the righteous who are in Thy tender keeping.

And as we mourn our people's tragic fate, we also recall with admiration and gratitude the compassionate men and women of other faiths and nationalities who, at the peril of their lives, protected and saved thousands of Jews.

> They are among those whom our Rabbis had in mind when they taught: "The righteous of all nations have a share in the world to come."

We are grateful to all the Allied Nations who liberated our people, and people of other faiths, from Nazi imprisonment, torture, and death.

> With thankful hearts we shall ever remember the care and encouragement they gave to all those who were tragically displaced.

Let us all pray and work together for that day when there shall be no more violence or desolation anywhere on this earth.

> "Nation shall not lift sword against nation; neither shall they learn war any more."

(Additional passages may be introduced here.)

FROM TRAGEDY TO TRIUMPH

We who have witnessed the darkest chapter in modern Jewish history, have also witnessed our people's greatest triumph: the rebirth of the Jewish State.

> We thank Thee, O Lord, that Thou hast permitted us to behold our people's return to Zion.

Thou hast opened the gates, and Thou didst "bring the remnant of Thy people from the east, and didst gather them from the west; Thou didst say to the north 'Give up!' and to the south 'Do not withhold them!'

> "Thou didst bring Thy sons from afar, and Thy daughters from the ends of the earth!"

May we who live in this land of freedom, help our brothers to rebuild the State of Israel, that it may become secure and self-supporting, a stronghold of democracy, a bridge which unites the peoples of the East and of the West.

> "For out of Zion shall go forth the Torah,
> And the word of God from Jerusalem."

(Additional passages may be introduced here.)

14. Hallel — Recite the Hallel — הַלֵּל

A Note on Making Selections: *In the* Hallel, *"Psalms of Praise" (pages 47-53) and in* Nishmat Kol Ḥai, *"A Poem of Praise" which follows it (pages 56-59), sections or excerpts may be selected for recitation.*

Alternate selections from both Hallel *and* Nishmat *may be utilized on each Seder night.*

Psalms of Praise (*Hallel*) precede and follow the festival meal, indicating that the meal is part of a religious service. In Judaism, the family meal is sanctified with prayer and words of Torah. The following Psalms constitute the "second part" of the Hallel. (The "first part," Psalms 113 and 114, was recited before the meal.)

TRUST IN THE LORD!

Psalm 115:1–11	תהלים קטו, א–יא
Not for our sake, O Lord, Not for our sake give glory, But to reveal Thy love and Thy truth.	לֹא לָנוּ, יְיָ, לֹא לָנוּ, כִּי לְשִׁמְךָ תֵּן כָּבוֹד, עַל חַסְדְּךָ, עַל אֲמִתֶּךָ.
Why should the nations taunt us, saying: "Where now is their God?"	לָמָּה יֹאמְרוּ הַגּוֹיִם, אַיֵּה נָא אֱלֹהֵיהֶם?
Our God is in the heavens, Doing whatsoever He desires.	וֵאלֹהֵינוּ בַשָּׁמָיִם; כֹּל אֲשֶׁר חָפֵץ עָשָׂה.
Their idols are mere silver and gold, The handiwork of men.	עֲצַבֵּיהֶם כֶּסֶף וְזָהָב, מַעֲשֵׂה יְדֵי אָדָם.
They have mouths, but they speak not; Eyes have they, but they see not.	פֶּה לָהֶם וְלֹא יְדַבֵּרוּ, עֵינַיִם לָהֶם וְלֹא יִרְאוּ.
They have ears, but they hear not; Noses have they, but they breathe not.	אָזְנַיִם לָהֶם וְלֹא יִשְׁמָעוּ, אַף לָהֶם וְלֹא יְרִיחוּן.
They have hands, but they touch not; Feet have they, but they walk not; Neither can they utter a sound with their throats.	יְדֵיהֶם וְלֹא יְמִישׁוּן, רַגְלֵיהֶם וְלֹא יְהַלֵּכוּ; לֹא יֶהְגּוּ בִּגְרוֹנָם.
Whoever makes them shall become like them; Yea, every one that trusts in them.	כְּמוֹהֶם יִהְיוּ עֹשֵׂיהֶם, כֹּל אֲשֶׁר בֹּטֵחַ בָּהֶם.
O Israel, trust in the Lord! He is your help and your shield.	יִשְׂרָאֵל, בְּטַח בַּייָ; עֶזְרָם וּמָגִנָּם הוּא.

House of Aaron, trust in the Lord!
He is your help and your shield.

בֵּית אַהֲרֹן, בִּטְחוּ בַיְיָ;
עֶזְרָם וּמָגִנָּם הוּא.

You who revere the Lord, trust in the Lord!
He is your help and your shield.

יִרְאֵי יְיָ, בִּטְחוּ בַייָ;
עֶזְרָם וּמָגִנָּם הוּא.

Only the Living Can Praise the Lord

Psalm 115:12–18

תהלים קטו, יב–יח

The Lord who has been mindful of us, will bless us;
He will bless the house of Israel;
He will bless the house of Aaron.

יְיָ זְכָרָנוּ יְבָרֵךְ;
יְבָרֵךְ אֶת בֵּית יִשְׂרָאֵל,
יְבָרֵךְ אֶת בֵּית אַהֲרֹן.

He will bless those who revere the Lord,
Both low and high alike.

יְבָרֵךְ יִרְאֵי יְיָ,
הַקְּטַנִּים עִם הַגְּדֹלִים.

May the Lord increase your numbers,
Yours and your children's.

יֹסֵף יְיָ עֲלֵיכֶם,
עֲלֵיכֶם וְעַל בְּנֵיכֶם.

Blessed may you be by the Lord,
Maker of heaven and earth.

בְּרוּכִים אַתֶּם לַייָ,
עֹשֵׂה שָׁמַיִם וָאָרֶץ.

The heavens are the heavens of the Lord,
But the earth has He given to the children of men.

הַשָּׁמַיִם שָׁמַיִם לַייָ,
וְהָאָרֶץ נָתַן לִבְנֵי אָדָם.

The dead cannot praise the Lord,
Nor do any that go down into silence.

לֹא הַמֵּתִים יְהַלְלוּ יָהּ,
וְלֹא כָּל יֹרְדֵי דוּמָה.

But we will praise the Lord,
From this time forth and forever.

וַאֲנַחְנוּ נְבָרֵךְ יָהּ
מֵעַתָּה וְעַד עוֹלָם;

Halleluyah!

הַלְלוּיָהּ!

THANKSGIVING FOR GOD'S MERCIES

Responsive Reading

Psalm 116	תהלים קטז
I delight when the Lord hears The voice of my supplications.	אָהַבְתִּי כִּי יִשְׁמַע יְיָ אֶת קוֹלִי תַּחֲנוּנָי.
Because He has inclined His ear unto me, Therefore will I call upon Him all my days.	כִּי הִטָּה אָזְנוֹ לִי, וּבְיָמַי אֶקְרָא.
The cords of death encircled me, And the fear of the grave seized me; I was in anguish and despair.	אֲפָפוּנִי חֶבְלֵי מָוֶת, וּמְצָרֵי שְׁאוֹל מְצָאוּנִי; צָרָה וְיָגוֹן אֶמְצָא.
Then I called upon the Lord: "O Lord, do Thou save me."	וּבְשֵׁם יְיָ אֶקְרָא, אָנָּה יְיָ, מַלְּטָה נַפְשִׁי.
Gracious is the Lord, and righteous; Yea, our God is merciful.	חַנּוּן יְיָ וְצַדִּיק, וֵאלֹהֵינוּ מְרַחֵם.
The Lord guards the simple; I was brought low and He saved me.	שֹׁמֵר פְּתָאִים יְיָ; דַּלֹּתִי וְלִי יְהוֹשִׁיעַ.
Regain your tranquility, O my soul, For the Lord has dealt bountifully with you,	שׁוּבִי נַפְשִׁי לִמְנוּחָיְכִי, כִּי יְיָ גָּמַל עָלָיְכִי.
For Thou, O Lord, hast delivered me from death, Mine eyes from tears, And my feet from stumbling.	כִּי חִלַּצְתָּ נַפְשִׁי מִמָּוֶת, אֶת עֵינִי מִן דִּמְעָה, אֶת רַגְלִי מִדֶּחִי.
I shall walk before the Lord In the land of the living.	אֶתְהַלֵּךְ לִפְנֵי יְיָ, בְּאַרְצוֹת הַחַיִּים.
I had faith even when I cried out: "I am greatly afflicted."	הֶאֱמַנְתִּי כִּי אֲדַבֵּר, אֲנִי עָנִיתִי מְאֹד.
And even when in panic I said: "All men are deceitful."	אֲנִי אָמַרְתִּי בְחָפְזִי, כָּל הָאָדָם כֹּזֵב.

What can I render unto the Lord,
For all His bounties to me?

מָה אָשִׁיב לַייָ
כָּל תַּגְמוּלוֹהִי עָלָי?

I will lift up the cup of salvation,
And call upon the name of the Lord.

כּוֹס יְשׁוּעוֹת אֶשָּׂא,
וּבְשֵׁם יְיָ אֶקְרָא.

My vows to the Lord will I fulfill,
In the presence of all His people.

נְדָרַי לַייָ אֲשַׁלֵּם,
נֶגְדָה נָּא לְכָל עַמּוֹ.

Grievous in the sight of the Lord
Is the death of His faithful ones.

יָקָר בְּעֵינֵי יְיָ
הַמָּוְתָה לַחֲסִידָיו.

Ah, Lord, I am indeed Thy servant;
I am Thy servant, the son of Thy handmaid;
Thou hast loosened my bonds.

אָנָּה יְיָ, כִּי אֲנִי עַבְדֶּךָ,
אֲנִי עַבְדְּךָ בֶּן אֲמָתֶךָ;
פִּתַּחְתָּ לְמוֹסֵרָי.

I will render Thee an offering of thanksgiving,
And will call upon the name of the Lord.

לְךָ אֶזְבַּח זֶבַח תּוֹדָה,
וּבְשֵׁם יְיָ אֶקְרָא.

My vows to the Lord will I fulfill,
In the presence of all His people,

נְדָרַי לַייָ אֲשַׁלֵּם,
נֶגְדָה נָּא לְכָל עַמּוֹ.

In the courts of the Lord's house,
In the midst of Jerusalem.

בְּחַצְרוֹת בֵּית יְיָ,
בְּתוֹכֵכִי יְרוּשָׁלָיִם;

Halleluyah!

הַלְלוּיָהּ!

GOD'S LOVINGKINDNESS IS EVERLASTING

Responsive Reading

PSALM 117

תהלים קיז

Praise the Lord, all nations;
Extol Him, all peoples.

הַלְלוּ אֶת יְיָ, כָּל גּוֹיִם;
שַׁבְּחוּהוּ, כָּל הָאֻמִּים.

For great is His kindness toward us;
And His faithfulness is everlasting.
Halleluyah!

כִּי גָבַר עָלֵינוּ חַסְדּוֹ,
וֶאֱמֶת יְיָ לְעוֹלָם;
הַלְלוּיָהּ!

Psalm 118

תהלים קיח

Give thanks to the Lord, for He is good,
His lovingkindness is everlasting.

הוֹדוּ לַייָ כִּי טוֹב
כִּי לְעוֹלָם חַסְדּוֹ.

Let Israel now proclaim,
That His lovingkindness is everlasting.

יֹאמַר נָא יִשְׂרָאֵל
כִּי לְעוֹלָם חַסְדּוֹ.

Let the house of Aaron proclaim,
That His lovingkindness is everlasting.

יֹאמְרוּ נָא בֵית אַהֲרֹן
כִּי לְעוֹלָם חַסְדּוֹ.

Let those who revere the Lord proclaim,
That His lovingkindness is everlasting.

יֹאמְרוּ נָא יִרְאֵי יְיָ
כִּי לְעוֹלָם חַסְדּוֹ.

Out of my distress I called upon the Lord;
He answered me and set me free.

מִן הַמֵּצַר קָרָאתִי יָּהּ,
עָנָנִי בַמֶּרְחָב יָהּ.

The Lord is with me, I will not fear;
What can man do to me?

יְיָ לִי, לֹא אִירָא;
מַה יַּעֲשֶׂה לִי אָדָם?

The Lord is with me as my helper;
I shall see the downfall of mine enemies,

יְיָ לִי בְּעֹזְרָי,
וַאֲנִי אֶרְאֶה בְשֹׂנְאָי.

It is better to rely upon the Lord
Than to depend upon man.

טוֹב לַחֲסוֹת בַּייָ
מִבְּטֹחַ בָּאָדָם.

It is better to rely upon the Lord
Than to depend upon princes.

טוֹב לַחֲסוֹת בַּייָ
מִבְּטֹחַ בִּנְדִיבִים.

Many nations encircled me;
In the name of the Lord I overcame them.

כָּל גּוֹיִם סְבָבוּנִי;
בְּשֵׁם יְיָ, כִּי אֲמִילַם.

They encircled me all around;
In the name of the Lord I overcame them.

סַבּוּנִי גַם סְבָבוּנִי;
בְּשֵׁם יְיָ, כִּי אֲמִילַם.

They swarmed about me like bees;
They were quenched as a fire among thorns;
In the name of the Lord I overcame them.

סַבּוּנִי כִדְבֹרִים,
דֹּעֲכוּ כְּאֵשׁ קוֹצִים;
בְּשֵׁם יְיָ, כִּי אֲמִילַם.

They thrust at me to make me fall; But the Lord came to my assistance.	דָּחֹה דְחִיתַנִי לִנְפֹּל, וַייָ עֲזָרָנִי.
The Lord is my strength and my song, And He has become my deliverance.	עָזִּי וְזִמְרָת יָהּ, וַיְהִי לִי לִישׁוּעָה.
Hark! This joyous song of victory Is heard in the tents of the righteous:	קוֹל רִנָּה וִישׁוּעָה בְּאָהֳלֵי צַדִּיקִים;
"The might of the Lord is triumphant! The power of the Lord is exalted! The strength of the Lord is victorious!"	יְמִין יְיָ עֹשָׂה חָיִל! יְמִין יְיָ רוֹמֵמָה! יְמִין יְיָ עֹשָׂה חָיִל!
I shall not die, but live To recount the works of the Lord.	לֹא אָמוּת כִּי אֶחְיֶה, וַאֲסַפֵּר מַעֲשֵׂי יָהּ.
The Lord has severely chastened me, But He has not given me over to death.	יַסֹּר יִסְּרַנִּי יָּהּ, וְלַמָּוֶת לֹא נְתָנָנִי.
Open to me the gates of righteousness, That I may enter and praise the Lord.	פִּתְחוּ לִי שַׁעֲרֵי צֶדֶק; אָבֹא בָם, אוֹדֶה יָהּ.
This is the gate of the Lord; The righteous alone shall enter.	זֶה הַשַּׁעַר לַייָ, צַדִּיקִים יָבֹאוּ בוֹ.

Each of the following verses is repeated.

I thank Thee, O Lord, that Thou hast answered me, And art become my deliverance.	אוֹדְךָ כִּי עֲנִיתָנִי, וַתְּהִי לִי לִישׁוּעָה.
The stone which the builders rejected Has become the chief cornerstone.	אֶבֶן מָאֲסוּ הַבּוֹנִים, הָיְתָה לְרֹאשׁ פִּנָּה.

This is the work of the Lord;
It is marvelous in our eyes.

מֵאֵת יְיָ הָיְתָה זֹּאת;
הִיא נִפְלָאת בְּעֵינֵינוּ.

This is the day which the Lord has made;
Let us rejoice and be glad thereon.

זֶה הַיּוֹם עָשָׂה יְיָ,
נָגִילָה וְנִשְׂמְחָה בוֹ.

We beseech Thee, O Lord, do Thou help us!
We beseech Thee, O Lord, do Thou prosper us!

אָנָּא יְיָ, הוֹשִׁיעָה נָּא.
אָנָּא יְיָ, הַצְלִיחָה נָא.

Blessed be he who comes in the name of the Lord;
We bless you from the house of the Lord.

בָּרוּךְ הַבָּא בְּשֵׁם יְיָ;
בֵּרַכְנוּכֶם מִבֵּית יְיָ.

The Lord is God; He has given us light;
Adorn the festival procession with myrtle boughs
To the very horns of the altar, (singing):

אֵל יְיָ וַיָּאֶר לָנוּ,
אִסְרוּ חַג בַּעֲבֹתִים,
עַד קַרְנוֹת הַמִּזְבֵּחַ.

"Thou art my God, and I will give thanks unto Thee;
Thou art my God; I will extol Thee.

אֵלִי אַתָּה וְאוֹדֶךָּ,
אֱלֹהַי אֲרוֹמְמֶךָּ.

Give thanks to the Lord, for He is good;
His lovingkindness is everlasting."

הוֹדוּ לַיְיָ כִּי טוֹב,
כִּי לְעוֹלָם חַסְדּוֹ.

Prayer Closing the Hallel

All Thy works shall praise Thee, O Lord our God, and Thy pious ones, the just who do Thy will, together with all Thy people, the house of Israel, shall praise Thee in joyous song. They shall thank, exalt, revere and sanctify Thee, and ascribe sovereignty to Thy name, O our King. For it is good to give thanks to Thee, and it is fitting to sing praises to Thy name, for Thou art God from everlasting to everlasting.

יְהַלְלוּךָ, יְיָ אֱלֹהֵינוּ, כָּל מַעֲשֶׂיךָ; וַחֲסִידֶיךָ, צַדִּיקִים עוֹשֵׂי רְצוֹנֶךָ, וְכָל עַמְּךָ בֵּית יִשְׂרָאֵל, בְּרִנָּה יוֹדוּ וִיבָרְכוּ, וִישַׁבְּחוּ וִיפָאֲרוּ, וִירוֹמְמוּ וְיַעֲרִיצוּ, וְיַקְדִּישׁוּ וְיַמְלִיכוּ אֶת שִׁמְךָ מַלְכֵּנוּ. כִּי לְךָ טוֹב לְהוֹדוֹת, וּלְשִׁמְךָ נָאֶה לְזַמֵּר, כִּי מֵעוֹלָם עַד עוֹלָם אַתָּה אֵל. בָּרוּךְ אַתָּה, יְיָ, מֶלֶךְ מְהֻלָּל בַּתִּשְׁבָּחוֹת.

הַלֵּל הַגָּדוֹל

HALLEL HA-GADOL

Kee L'olam Ḥasdo. כִּי לְעוֹלָם חַסְדּוֹ.

Psalm 136

Give thanks to the Lord, for He is good;
His lovingkindness is everlasting.

Give thanks to the supreme God;
Give thanks to the supreme Lord;
His lovingkindness is everlasting.

Give thanks to Him alone who performs great wonders;
Whose wisdom made the heavens,
Who spread the earth over the waters,
And who made the heavenly lights,
The sun to rule by day,
The moon and the stars to rule by night;
His lovingkindness is everlasting.

He smote Egypt through their first-born,
And brought out Israel from among them,
With a strong hand and an outstretched arm;
His lovingkindness is everlasting.

He divided the Red Sea,
And led Israel safely through it;
But He overthrew Pharaoh and his army in the Red Sea.
He led His people through the wilderness;
His lovingkindness is everlasting.

He smote great kings who oppressed us,
And struck down these mighty kings:
Sihon, king of the Amorites,
And Og, king of Bashan,

תהלים קלו

הוֹדוּ לַיְיָ, כִּי טוֹב,
כִּי לְעוֹלָם חַסְדּוֹ.

הוֹדוּ לֵאלֹהֵי הָאֱלֹהִים, כִּלְ״חַ.
הוֹדוּ לַאֲדֹנֵי הָאֲדֹנִים, כִּלְ״חַ.
לְעֹשֵׂה נִפְלָאוֹת גְּדֹלוֹת לְבַדּוֹ, כִּלְ״חַ.
לְעֹשֵׂה הַשָּׁמַיִם בִּתְבוּנָה, כִּלְ״חַ.
לְרוֹקַע הָאָרֶץ עַל הַמָּיִם, כִּלְ״חַ.
לְעֹשֵׂה אוֹרִים גְּדֹלִים, כִּלְ״חַ.
אֶת הַשֶּׁמֶשׁ לְמֶמְשֶׁלֶת בַּיּוֹם, כִּלְ״חַ.
אֶת הַיָּרֵחַ וְכוֹכָבִים לְמֶמְשְׁלוֹת בַּלָּיְלָה, כִּלְ״חַ.
לְמַכֵּה מִצְרַיִם בִּבְכוֹרֵיהֶם, כִּלְ״חַ.
וַיּוֹצֵא יִשְׂרָאֵל מִתּוֹכָם, כִּלְ״חַ.
בְּיָד חֲזָקָה וּבִזְרוֹעַ נְטוּיָה, כִּלְ״חַ.
לְגֹזֵר יַם סוּף לִגְזָרִים, כִּלְ״חַ.
וְהֶעֱבִיר יִשְׂרָאֵל בְּתוֹכוֹ, כִּלְ״חַ.
וְנִעֵר פַּרְעֹה וְחֵילוֹ בְיַם סוּף, כִּלְ״חַ.
לְמוֹלִיךְ עַמּוֹ בַּמִּדְבָּר, כִּלְ״חַ.
לְמַכֵּה מְלָכִים גְּדֹלִים, כִּלְ״חַ.
וַיַּהֲרֹג מְלָכִים אַדִּירִים, כִּלְ״חַ.
לְסִיחוֹן מֶלֶךְ הָאֱמֹרִי, כִּלְ״חַ.
וּלְעוֹג מֶלֶךְ הַבָּשָׁן, כִּלְ״חַ.

And He gave their land as a heritage,
A heritage to Israel, His servant;
His lovingkindness is everlasting.

He remembered us when we were downcast,
And redeemed us from our foes;
His lovingkindness is everlasting.

He gives food to all creatures;
His lovingkindness is everlasting.

Give thanks to the God of heaven;

His lovingkindness is everlasting.

וְנָתַן אַרְצָם לְנַחֲלָה, כְּלְ״חַ.
נַחֲלָה לְיִשְׂרָאֵל עַבְדּוֹ, כְּלְ״חַ.
שֶׁבְּשִׁפְלֵנוּ זָכַר לָנוּ, כְּלְ״חַ.
וַיִּפְרְקֵנוּ מִצָּרֵינוּ, כְּלְ״חַ.
נֹתֵן לֶחֶם לְכָל בָּשָׂר, כְּלְ״חַ.

הוֹדוּ לְאֵל הַשָּׁמָיִם,
כִּי לְעוֹלָם חַסְדּוֹ.

NISHMAT: A Service of Praise — *pages 56 through 59.*

(See "Note on Making Selections," page 47.)

שְׁמַת כָּל חַי תְּבָרֵךְ אֶת
שִׁמְךָ, יְיָ אֱלֹהֵינוּ, וְרוּחַ
כָּל בָּשָׂר תְּפָאֵר וּתְרוֹמֵם
זִכְרְךָ, מַלְכֵּנוּ, תָּמִיד. מִן הָעוֹלָם
וְעַד הָעוֹלָם אַתָּה אֵל, וּמִבַּלְעָדֶיךָ
אֵין לָנוּ מֶלֶךְ גּוֹאֵל וּמוֹשִׁיעַ, פּוֹדֶה
וּמַצִּיל וּמְפַרְנֵס, וּמְרַחֵם בְּכָל עֵת
צָרָה וְצוּקָה; אֵין לָנוּ מֶלֶךְ אֶלָּא
אָתָּה.

אֱלֹהֵי הָרִאשׁוֹנִים וְהָאַחֲרוֹנִים,
אֱלוֹהַּ כָּל בְּרִיּוֹת, אֲדוֹן כָּל תּוֹלָדוֹת,
הַמְהֻלָּל בְּרֹב הַתִּשְׁבָּחוֹת, הַמְנַהֵג
עוֹלָמוֹ בְּחֶסֶד וּבְרִיּוֹתָיו בְּרַחֲמִים.
וַיְיָ לֹא יָנוּם וְלֹא יִישָׁן, הַמְעוֹרֵר
יְשֵׁנִים, וְהַמֵּקִיץ נִרְדָּמִים, וְהַמֵּשִׂיחַ
אִלְּמִים, וְהַמַּתִּיר אֲסוּרִים, וְהַסּוֹמֵךְ
נוֹפְלִים, וְהַזּוֹקֵף כְּפוּפִים. לְךָ לְבַדְּךָ
אֲנַחְנוּ מוֹדִים.

אִלּוּ פִינוּ מָלֵא שִׁירָה כַּיָּם, וּלְשׁוֹנֵנוּ
רִנָּה כַּהֲמוֹן גַּלָּיו, וְשִׂפְתוֹתֵינוּ שֶׁבַח
כְּמֶרְחֲבֵי רָקִיעַ, וְעֵינֵינוּ מְאִירוֹת
כַּשֶּׁמֶשׁ וְכַיָּרֵחַ, וְיָדֵינוּ פְרוּשׂוֹת כְּנִשְׁרֵי

All things that live shall praise Thy name,
The spirit of all flesh proclaim
Thy sovereignty, O Lord our God.

From everlasting Thou art God,
To everlasting Thou shalt be;
We have no other God but Thee.

Thy goodness and Thy holiness
Support us in all times of stress,
Redeemer, Lord and King.

Thou art the God of first and last,
In every age Thy children raise
Their voices in eternal praise.

With tender love Thy world dost guide,
And for our needs dost Thou provide;
Thou keepest watch eternally.

Thou takest slumber from our eyes,
And to the speechless givest voice;
Through Thy great mercy all rejoice.

Thou raisest those whose heads are bent,
Sustaining all the weak and spent;
To Thee alone we render thanks.

If like the sea our mouths could sing,
Our tongues like murmuring waves implore,
Our lips like spacious skies adore;

And were our eyes like moon or sun,
Our hands like eagles' wings upon
The heavens, to spread and reach to Thee;

And if our feet were swift as hinds,
Yet would we still unable be
To thank Thee, God, sufficiently;

To thank Thee for one-thousandth share
Of all Thy kind and loving care
Which Thou in every age hast shown.

From Egypt didst Thou lead us forth,
From bondage didst Thou set us free,
Redeeming us from slavery.

In famine, food didst Thou provide,
In plenty, Thou wast at our side,
To keep and guide us, Lord our God.

From pestilence and sword didst save,
And when we were by ills assailed,
Thy love and mercy never failed.

O Lord, Thy wondrous deeds we praise,
Forsake us not throughout our days;
Be Thou our help forevermore.

Therefore, O Lord, our limbs, our breath,
Our soul, our tongue, shall all proclaim
Thy praise, and glorify Thy name;

And every mouth and every tongue
Declare allegiance without end;
And every knee to Thee shall bend.

The mighty ones shall humble be,
Yea, every heart revere but Thee,
And sing the glory of Thy name.

שָׁמָיִם, וְרַגְלֵינוּ קַלּוֹת כָּאַיָּלוֹת, אֵין אֲנַחְנוּ מַסְפִּיקִים לְהוֹדוֹת לְךָ, יְיָ אֱלֹהֵינוּ וֵאלֹהֵי אֲבוֹתֵינוּ, וּלְבָרֵךְ אֶת שִׁמְךָ עַל אַחַת מֵאֶלֶף (אֶלֶף) אַלְפֵי אֲלָפִים וְרִבֵּי רְבָבוֹת פְּעָמִים הַטּוֹבוֹת שֶׁעָשִׂיתָ עִם אֲבוֹתֵינוּ וְעִמָּנוּ. מִמִּצְרַיִם גְּאַלְתָּנוּ, יְיָ אֱלֹהֵינוּ, וּמִבֵּית עֲבָדִים פְּדִיתָנוּ; בְּרָעָב זַנְתָּנוּ וּבְשָׂבָע כִּלְכַּלְתָּנוּ; מֵחֶרֶב הִצַּלְתָּנוּ וּמִדֶּבֶר מִלַּטְתָּנוּ, וּמֵחֳלָיִם רָעִים וְנֶאֱמָנִים דִּלִּיתָנוּ.

עַד הֵנָּה עֲזָרוּנוּ רַחֲמֶיךָ וְלֹא עֲזָבוּנוּ חֲסָדֶיךָ; וְאַל תִּטְּשֵׁנוּ, יְיָ אֱלֹהֵינוּ, לָנֶצַח. עַל כֵּן, אֵבָרִים שֶׁפִּלַּגְתָּ בָּנוּ, וְרוּחַ וּנְשָׁמָה שֶׁנָּפַחְתָּ בְּאַפֵּינוּ, וְלָשׁוֹן אֲשֶׁר שַׂמְתָּ בְּפִינוּ, הֵן הֵם יוֹדוּ וִיבָרְכוּ, וִישַׁבְּחוּ וִיפָאֲרוּ, וִירוֹמְמוּ וְיַעֲרִיצוּ, וְיַקְדִּישׁוּ וְיַמְלִיכוּ אֶת שִׁמְךָ, מַלְכֵּנוּ. כִּי כָל פֶּה לְךָ יוֹדֶה, וְכָל לָשׁוֹן לְךָ תִשָּׁבַע, וְכָל בֶּרֶךְ לְךָ תִכְרַע, וְכָל קוֹמָה לְפָנֶיךָ תִשְׁתַּחֲוֶה. וְכָל לְבָבוֹת יִירָאוּךָ, וְכָל קֶרֶב וּכְלָיוֹת יְזַמְּרוּ לִשְׁמֶךָ, כַּדָּבָר

שֶׁכָּתוּב: כָּל עַצְמוֹתַי תֹּאמַרְנָה, יְיָ מִי כָמוֹךָ? מַצִּיל עָנִי מֵחָזָק מִמֶּנּוּ, וְעָנִי וְאֶבְיוֹן מִגֹּזְלוֹ. מִי יִדְמֶה לָּךְ, וּמִי יִשְׁוֶה לָּךְ, וּמִי יַעֲרָךְ לָךְ, הָאֵל הַגָּדוֹל, הַגִּבּוֹר וְהַנּוֹרָא, אֵל עֶלְיוֹן, קֹנֵה שָׁמַיִם וָאָרֶץ? נְהַלֶּלְךָ וּנְשַׁבֵּחֲךָ וּנְפָאֶרְךָ, וּנְבָרֵךְ אֶת שֵׁם קָדְשֶׁךָ, כָּאָמוּר: לְדָוִד, בָּרְכִי נַפְשִׁי אֶת יְיָ, וְכָל קְרָבַי אֶת שֵׁם קָדְשׁוֹ.

In the words of the Psalmist: "My whole being shall proclaim: 'O Lord, who is like Thee? Thou deliverest the weak from him who is stronger, the poor and the needy from his despoiler.'" (35:10)

Who is like Thee, who is equal to Thee, who can be compared to Thee, O great, mighty, revered and supreme God, Creator of heaven and earth? We will praise, laud, and glorify Thee; we will extol Thy holy name in the words of the Psalm of David: "Praise the Lord, O my soul, and all that is within me, praise His holy name." (103:1)

הָאֵל בְּתַעֲצֻמוֹת עֻזֶּךָ, הַגָּדוֹל בִּכְבוֹד שְׁמֶךָ, הַגִּבּוֹר לָנֶצַח וְהַנּוֹרָא בְּנוֹרְאוֹתֶיךָ, הַמֶּלֶךְ הַיּוֹשֵׁב עַל כִּסֵּא רָם וְנִשָּׂא.

Thou art God by the power of Thy might; Thou art great by the glory of Thy name; Thou art mighty unto everlasting, and revered for Thine awe-inspiring works; Thou art King, enthroned on high.

שׁוֹכֵן עַד, מָרוֹם וְקָדוֹשׁ שְׁמוֹ. וְכָתוּב: רַנְּנוּ צַדִּיקִים בַּייָ, לַיְשָׁרִים נָאוָה תְהִלָּה.

Thou who abidest in eternity, Thy name is "Exalted and Holy." As the Psalmist declared: "Rejoice in the Lord, O ye righteous; it is befitting for the upright to praise Him." (33:1)

בְּפִי יְשָׁרִים תִּתְהַלָּל,
וּבְדִבְרֵי צַדִּיקִים תִּתְבָּרַךְ,
וּבִלְשׁוֹן חֲסִידִים תִּתְרוֹמָם,
וּבְקֶרֶב קְדוֹשִׁים תִּתְקַדָּשׁ.

By the mouth of the upright,
Thou shalt be glorified;
By the words of the righteous,
Thou shalt be praised;
By the tongue of the faithful,
Thou shalt be extolled;
And in the midst of the holy,
Thou shalt be sanctified.

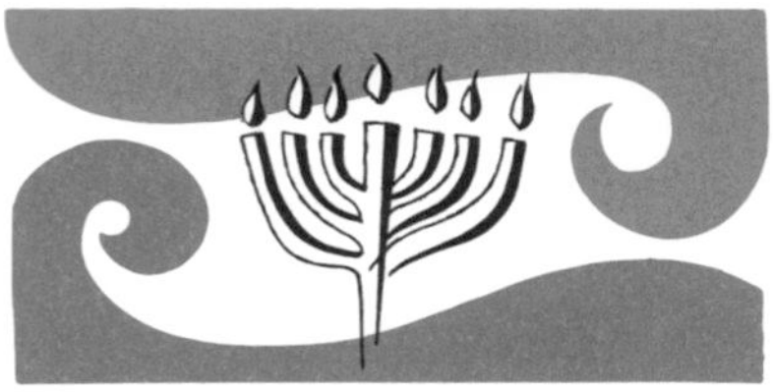

In the assembled multitudes of Thy people, the house of Israel, Thy name, O our King, shall be glorified with song in every generation. For it is the duty of all creatures, O Lord our God and God of our ancestors, to thank, laud, adore and praise Thee, even beyond all the words of song and praise uttered by David, son of Jesse, Thine anointed servant.

וּבְמַקְהֲלוֹת רִבְבוֹת עַמְּךָ בֵּית יִשְׂרָאֵל בְּרִנָּה יִתְפָּאַר שִׁמְךָ, מַלְכֵּנוּ, בְּכָל דּוֹר וָדוֹר; שֶׁכֵּן חוֹבַת כָּל הַיְצוּרִים לְפָנֶיךָ, יְיָ אֱלֹהֵינוּ וֵאלֹהֵי אֲבוֹתֵינוּ, לְהוֹדוֹת, לְהַלֵּל, לְשַׁבֵּחַ, לְפָאֵר, לְרוֹמֵם, לְהַדֵּר, לְבָרֵךְ, לְעַלֵּה וּלְקַלֵּס עַל כָּל דִּבְרֵי שִׁירוֹת וְתִשְׁבְּחוֹת דָּוִד בֶּן יִשַׁי עַבְדְּךָ מְשִׁיחֶךָ.

Praised be Thy name forever, O our King, our divine Sovereign, great and holy in heaven and on earth. For to Thee are due, O Lord our God and God of our ancestors, song and praise, hymn and psalm, acclaiming Thy power and dominion, victory and glory, holiness and sovereignty. To Thee we offer praise and thanksgiving from this time forth and forevermore. Praised be Thou, exalted God, our King, to whom our thanks are due; Lord of wondrous deeds, who delightest in hymns of praise, Thou art God and King, the life of the universe.

יִשְׁתַּבַּח שִׁמְךָ לָעַד, מַלְכֵּנוּ, הָאֵל הַמֶּלֶךְ הַגָּדוֹל וְהַקָּדוֹשׁ, בַּשָּׁמַיִם וּבָאָרֶץ. כִּי לְךָ נָאֶה, יְיָ אֱלֹהֵינוּ וֵאלֹהֵי אֲבוֹתֵינוּ, שִׁיר וּשְׁבָחָה, הַלֵּל וְזִמְרָה, עֹז וּמֶמְשָׁלָה, נֶצַח, גְּדֻלָּה וּגְבוּרָה, תְּהִלָּה וְתִפְאֶרֶת, קְדֻשָּׁה וּמַלְכוּת, בְּרָכוֹת וְהוֹדָאוֹת, מֵעַתָּה וְעַד עוֹלָם. בָּרוּךְ אַתָּה, יְיָ, אֵל מֶלֶךְ גָּדוֹל בַּתִּשְׁבָּחוֹת, אֵל הַהוֹדָאוֹת, אֲדוֹן הַנִּפְלָאוֹת, הַבּוֹחֵר בְּשִׁירֵי זִמְרָה, מֶלֶךְ, אֵל, חֵי הָעוֹלָמִים.

For the First Seder Night (Optional)

The following PIYYUT (poem) in alphabetical acrostic was probably composed in the seventh century by Rabbi Yannai. The poet fancifully enumerates miracles in Biblical history which, according to tradition, occurred at midnight. He concludes with the hope of ultimate redemption, to take place on Passover night. The refrain, "It came to pass at midnight," is from Exodus 12:29.

And it Came to Pass at Midnight.

וּבְכֵן, וַיְהִי בַּחֲצִי הַלַּיְלָה.

In the days of old didst Thou perform many miracles at night.
In the early watch of evening, on this night,
To gain the victory, Abraham divided his army at night. (Gen. 14:15)
And it came to pass at midnight.

אָז רוֹב נִסִּים הִפְלֵאתָ בַּלַּיְלָה,
בְּרֹאשׁ אַשְׁמוּרוֹת זֶה הַלַּיְלָה,
גֵּר צֶדֶק נִצַּחְתּוֹ כְּנֶחֱלַק לוֹ לַיְלָה.
וַיְהִי בַּחֲצִי הַלַּיְלָה.

Thou didst judge Abimelech, king of Gerar, in a dream during the night; (Gen. 20:3)
Thou didst strike Laban, the Syrian, with terror in the night; (Gen. 31:24)
Israel wrestled with an angel, and prevailed at night. (Gen. 32:25)
And it came to pass at midnight.

דַּנְתָּ מֶלֶךְ גְּרָר בַּחֲלוֹם הַלַּיְלָה,
הִפְחַדְתָּ אֲרַמִּי בְּאֶמֶשׁ לַיְלָה,
וַיָּשַׂר יִשְׂרָאֵל לְמַלְאָךְ וַיּוּכַל לוֹ לַיְלָה.
וַיְהִי בַּחֲצִי הַלַּיְלָה.

Egypt's first-born didst Thou smite at night; (Ex. 12:29)
The Egyptians found themselves powerless when they arose at night.
Sisera's army didst Thou scatter, aided by the stars of night. (Judg. 5:20)
It came to pass at midnight.

זֶרַע בְּכוֹרֵי פַתְרוֹס מָחַצְתָּ בַּחֲצִי הַלַּיְלָה,
חֵילָם לֹא מָצְאוּ בְּקוּמָם בַּלַּיְלָה,
טִיסַת נְגִיד חֲרֹשֶׁת סִלִּיתָ בְּכוֹכְבֵי לַיְלָה.
וַיְהִי בַּחֲצִי הַלַּיְלָה.

Sennacherib's army was decimated at night; (2 Ki. 19:35)
Babylonia's god, Bel, and his pillar crashed in the night; (Is. 46:1, 2)
Mysteries were revealed to Daniel in a vision at night. (Dan. 2:19)
It came to pass at midnight.

יָעַץ מְחָרֵף לְנוֹפֵף אִוּוּי הוֹבַשְׁתָּ פְגָרָיו בַּלַּיְלָה,
כָּרַע בֵּל וּמַצָּבוֹ בְּאִישׁוֹן לַיְלָה,
לְאִישׁ חֲמוּדוֹת נִגְלָה רָז חֲזוֹת לַיְלָה.
וַיְהִי בַּחֲצִי הַלַּיְלָה.

Drunken Balshazzar was slain at night; (Dan. 5:30)
Daniel, saved from the lions' den, interpreted the dreams of night. (Dan. 6:24)
Hateful Haman wrote his edicts at night. (Esth. 3:12)
It came to pass at midnight.

מִשְׁתַּכֵּר בִּכְלֵי קֹדֶשׁ נֶהֱרַג בּוֹ בַּלַּיְלָה,
נוֹשַׁע מִבּוֹר אֲרָיוֹת פּוֹתֵר בִּעֲתוּתֵי לַיְלָה,
שִׂנְאָה נָטַר אֲגָגִי וְכָתַב סְפָרִים בַּלַּיְלָה.
וַיְהִי בַּחֲצִי הַלַּיְלָה.

Thou didst triumph over Haman when sleep failed Ahasuerus at night. (Esth. 6:1)
Thou didst tread down the enemy for him who asked: "Watchman, what of the night?" (Is. 63:3; 21:11)
Thou wilt answer like the watchman: "The morning comes as well as the night." (Is. 21:12)
It came to pass at midnight.

ע וֹרַרְתָּ נִצְחֲךָ עָלָיו בְּנֶדֶד שְׁנַת לַיְלָה,
פּ וּרָה תִדְרוֹךְ לְשׁוֹמֵר מַה מִּלַּיְלָה,
צָ רַח כַּשּׁוֹמֵר וְשָׂח אָתָא בֹקֶר וְגַם לַיְלָה.
וַיְהִי בַּחֲצִי הַלַּיְלָה.

Hasten that day which is neither day nor night; (Zech. 14:7)
Most High, proclaim that Thine is the day, and Thine is also the night.
Place watchmen to guard the city, day and night. (Is. 62:6)
Make bright as day the darkness of the night.
May it come to pass at midnight.

קָ רֵב יוֹם אֲשֶׁר הוּא לֹא יוֹם וְלֹא לַיְלָה,
רָ ם הוֹדַע כִּי לְךָ הַיּוֹם אַף לְךָ הַלַּיְלָה,
שׁ וֹמְרִים הַפְקֵד לְעִירְךָ כָּל הַיּוֹם וְכָל הַלַּיְלָה,
תָּ אִיר כְּאוֹר יוֹם חֶשְׁכַת לַיְלָה.
וִיהִי בַּחֲצִי הַלַּיְלָה.

For the Second Seder Night (Optional)

The following PIYYUT, in alphabetical acrostic, written in the eighth century by Rabbi Eleazar Ha-Kalir, a pupil of Rabbi Yannai, recounts the various deliverances that, according to Midrashic interpretation, took place at the Passover season. The refrain, "This is the Offering of Passover," is from Exodus 12:27.

You shall say:

This is the offering of Passover.

וּבְכֵן,

וַאֲמַרְתֶּם זֶבַח פֶּסַח.

The power of Thy might Thou didst reveal on Passover;
Above all other festivals didst Thou place the Passover;
To Abraham Thou didst reveal the midnight marvels of the Passover. (Baba Bathra 15a)
This is the offering of Passover.

אֹ מֶץ גְּבוּרוֹתֶיךָ הִפְלֵאתָ בַּפֶּסַח,
בְּ רֹאשׁ כָּל מוֹעֲדוֹת נִשֵּׂאתָ פֶּסַח,
גִּ לִּיתָ לְאֶזְרָחִי חֲצוֹת לֵיל פֶּסַח.
וַאֲמַרְתֶּם זֶבַח פֶּסַח.

To his door Thou didst come at midday's heat on Passover;
He served the angels with unleavened bread on Passover;
And to the herd he ran, to fetch a calf for Passover. (Gen. 18:1, 6, 7)
This is the offering of Passover.

דְּ לָתָיו דָּפַקְתָּ כְּחֹם הַיּוֹם בַּפֶּסַח,
הִ סְעִיד נוֹצְצִים עֻגוֹת מַצּוֹת בַּפֶּסַח,
וְ אֶל הַבָּקָר רָץ זֵכֶר לְשׁוֹר עֵרֶךְ פֶּסַח.
וַאֲמַרְתֶּם זֶבַח פֶּסַח.

The wicked men of Sodom were consumed by fire on Passover;
But Lot was saved, and baked unleavened bread on Passover. (Gen. 19:3)
Thou didst sweep away the power of Egypt on Passover.
This is the offering of Passover.

ז עֲמוּ סְדוֹמִים וְלֹהֲטוּ בָאֵשׁ בַּפֶּסַח,
חֻ לַּץ לוֹט מֵהֶם וּמַצּוֹת אָפָה בְּקֵץ פֶּסַח,
טִ אטֵאתָ אַדְמַת מֹף וְנֹף בְּעָבְרְךָ בַּפֶּסַח.
וַאֲמַרְתֶּם זֶבַח פֶּסַח.

O Lord, Thou didst smite the first-born of Egypt on the night of Passover;
O Mighty One, Thy first-born didst Thou spare on Passover;
Death passed over Israel's marked doors on Passover. (Ex. 12:23)
This is the offering of Passover.

יָ הּ רֹאשׁ כָּל אוֹן מָחַצְתָּ בְּלֵיל שִׁמּוּר פֶּסַח,
כַּ בִּיר עַל בֵּן בְּכוֹר פָּסַחְתָּ בְּדַם פֶּסַח,
לְ בִלְתִּי תֵּת מַשְׁחִית לָבֹא בִּפְתָחַי בַּפֶּסַח.
וַאֲמַרְתֶּם זֶבַח פֶּסַח.

The walled city of Jericho crashed on Passover. (Josh. 6:5)
Through a dream of barley cake, Midian was destroyed on Passover. (Judg. 7:13)
The mighty Assyrian hordes were consumed in blazing flame on Passover. (Midrash Yal. Shim.)
This is the offering of Passover.

מְ סֻגֶּרֶת סֻגָּרָה בְּעִתּוֹתֵי פֶּסַח,
נִ שְׁמְדָה מִדְיָן בִּצְלִיל שְׂעוֹרֵי עֹמֶר פֶּסַח,
שֹׂ רְפוּ מִשְׁמַנֵּי פּוּל וְלוּד בִּיקַד יְקוֹד פֶּסַח.
וַאֲמַרְתֶּם זֶבַח פֶּסַח.

Sennacherib, at Zion's gate, met disaster on Passover. (Is. 10:32)
Upon the wall, a hand wrote Babylon's fate on Passover. (Dan. 5:24)
"The watch is set; the table is spread" — (Is. 21:5)
Feasting Babylon met her doom on Passover.
This is the offering of Passover.

ע וֹד הַיּוֹם בְּנֹב לַעֲמוֹד עַד גָּעָה עוֹנַת פֶּסַח,
פַּ ס יָד כָּתְבָה לְקַעֲקֵעַ צוּל בַּפֶּסַח,
צָ פֹה הַצָּפִית עָרוֹךְ הַשֻּׁלְחָן בַּפֶּסַח.
וַאֲמַרְתֶּם זֶבַח פֶּסַח.

A three-day fast Queen Esther imposed on Passover. (Esth. 4:16)
The wicked Haman was hung on gallows fifty cubits high on Passover. (Esth. 7:9)
A double punishment shalt Thou bring upon our foes on Passover. (Is. 47:9)
Thy hand is strong, Thy right hand uplifted, Thy might shall again prevail on Passover. (Ps. 89:14)
This is the offering of Passover.

קָ הָל כִּנְּסָה הֲדַסָּה צוֹם לְשַׁלֵּשׁ בַּפֶּסַח,
ר אשׁ מִבֵּית רָשָׁע מָחַצְתָּ בְּעֵץ חֲמִשִּׁים בַּפֶּסַח,
שְׁ תֵּי אֵלֶּה רֶגַע תָּבִיא לְעוּצִית בַּפֶּסַח,
תָּ עֹז יָדְךָ תָּרוּם יְמִינְךָ כְּלֵיל הִתְקַדֵּשׁ חַג פֶּסַח.
וַאֲמַרְתֶּם זֶבַח פֶּסַח.

For the Second Seder Night

Sefirah — Counting the Omer — סְפִירָה

The custom of "counting the days" for seven weeks—from the second night of Passover until Shavuot—recalls the agricultural life of our people in ancient times. Each year, on the second day of Passover, they brought to the Sanctuary a measure (OMER) of their first barley harvest. (Lev. 23:10, 15, 16; Deut. 16:9)

According to Midrashic lore, the Israelites were told that fifty days after their liberation, they would receive the Torah on Mount Sinai. Just as one impatiently counts the days before a birthday, a wedding, or any other happy event, the Israelites, eagerly anticipating this occasion, began to count the days, saying each day: "Now there is one day less to wait before we receive the Torah."

The Biblical ordinance "to count days for seven weeks" (from Passover to Shavuot, the festival which commemorates the giving of the Torah), created a "bridge" connecting the two festivals. Our Sages stressed not only freedom *from* bondage, but freedom *for* a purpose. Freedom is not enough. It must lead to Torah. Without Law, freedom cannot endure. The linking of the Exodus and the giving of the Torah, emphasizes the nexus between freedom and moral law.

Over the centuries, the OMER observance strengthened our people's identification with the soil of the Holy Land—and their resolve, in modern times, to work for the rebuilding of Zion.

Praised be Thou, O Lord our God, King of the universe, who hast sanctified us with Thy commandments and enjoined upon us the mitzvah of counting the OMER.

בָּרוּךְ אַתָּה, יְיָ אֱלֹהֵינוּ, מֶלֶךְ הָעוֹלָם, אֲשֶׁר קִדְּשָׁנוּ בְּמִצְוֹתָיו וְצִוָּנוּ עַל סְפִירַת הָעֹמֶר:

This is the first day of the OMER.

הַיּוֹם יוֹם אֶחָד לָעֹמֶר:

Baruḥ atta Adonai, eloheynu meleḥ ha-olam,
asher kid-shanu b'mitzvo-tav, ve-tzivanu al se-firat ha-omer.
Ha-yom yom eḥad la-omer!

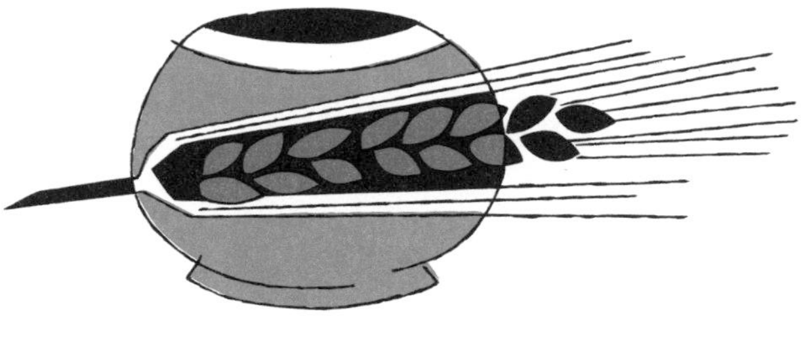

יְהִי רָצוֹן מִלְּפָנֶיךָ, יְיָ אֱלֹהֵינוּ וֵאלֹהֵי אֲבוֹתֵינוּ, שֶׁיִּבָּנֶה בֵּית הַמִּקְדָּשׁ בִּמְהֵרָה בְיָמֵינוּ. וְתֵן חֶלְקֵנוּ בְּתוֹרָתֶךָ:

The Four Cups of Wine

There are various explanations for the four cups of wine at the Seder . . .

The four cups correspond to the four letters of God's name: YOD HEH VAV HEH (Jehovah)—to indicate that God, the Liberator, is the Author of our freedom.

The four cups correspond to the four major divisions of the Seder service: The Kiddush; the reading of the Haggadah; the BIRKAT HAMAZON (Grace After Meals); and the concluding psalms and prayers.

The Bible uses four different expressions for the redemption of the Israelites from Egyptian bondage:

1. וְהוֹצֵאתִי — V'HO-TZE-TI, "*and I will bring you out* from under the burdens of the Egyptians."
2. וְהִצַּלְתִּי — V'HI-TZAL-TI, "*and I will deliver you* from their bondage."
3. וְגָאַלְתִּי — V'GA-AL-TI, "*and I will redeem you* with an outstretched arm, and with great judgments."
4. וְלָקַחְתִּי — V'LA-KAḤ-TI, "*and I will take you* to Me for a people." (Ex. 6:6, 7)

These four expressions have been interpreted to refer to political, economic, intellectual, and spiritual freedom. To be truly free, and to reach our highest potential, we must be free from want; free from all forms of oppression and tyranny; free in mind and spirit; and free to develop all the gifts with which God has endowed us.

After reciting the following blessing, drink the fourth cup of wine while reclining.

ברוך אתה יי אלהינו מלך העולם בורא פרי הגפן:

בָּרוּךְ אַתָּה, יְיָ אֱלֹהֵינוּ, מֶלֶךְ הָעוֹלָם, בּוֹרֵא פְּרִי הַגָּפֶן.

Baruḥ atta Adonai, eloheynu meleḥ ha-olam, boray p'ri ha-gafen.

Praised be Thou, O Lord our God, King of the Universe,
Creator of the Fruit of the Vine.

On Sabbath add words in brackets.

רוּךְ אַתָּה, יְיָ אֱלֹהֵינוּ,
מֶלֶךְ הָעוֹלָם, עַל הַגֶּפֶן
וְעַל פְּרִי הַגֶּפֶן, וְעַל
תְּנוּבַת הַשָּׂדֶה, וְעַל אֶרֶץ חֶמְדָּה
טוֹבָה וּרְחָבָה שֶׁרָצִיתָ וְהִנְחַלְתָּ
לַאֲבוֹתֵינוּ לֶאֱכֹל מִפִּרְיָהּ וְלִשְׂבֹּעַ
מִטּוּבָהּ. רַחֵם נָא, יְיָ אֱלֹהֵינוּ, עַל
יִשְׂרָאֵל עַמֶּךָ, וְעַל יְרוּשָׁלַיִם עִירֶךָ,
וְעַל צִיּוֹן מִשְׁכַּן כְּבוֹדֶךָ, וְעַל מִזְבְּחֶךָ

Praised be Thou, O Lord our God, King of the universe, for the vine and for the fruit of the vine, for the produce of the field and for the pleasant and spacious land which Thou, in Thy favor, didst grant to our ancestors as an inheritance that they might eat of its fruit and enjoy its bounty. Remember in mercy, O Lord our God, Israel Thy people, Jerusalem Thy city, Zion the abode of Thy glory, and Thy Temple. Rebuild

Jerusalem the holy city, speedily and in our lifetime. Lead us there and make us rejoice in its re-establishment, that we may eat of its fruit and enjoy its blessings so that we may praise Thee there in holiness and purity. [May it be Thy will to strengthen us on the Sabbath day.] Make us rejoice on this Festival of Unleavened Bread. For to Thee, O Lord, who art good and beneficent to all, we give thanks for that land and for the fruit of its vine. Praised be Thou, O Lord, for the land and for the fruit of the vine.

וְעַל הֵיכָלֶךָ. וּבְנֵה יְרוּשָׁלַיִם עִיר הַקֹּדֶשׁ בִּמְהֵרָה בְיָמֵינוּ, וְהַעֲלֵנוּ לְתוֹכָהּ וְשַׂמְּחֵנוּ בְּבִנְיָנָהּ, וְנֹאכַל מִפִּרְיָהּ וְנִשְׂבַּע מִטּוּבָהּ, וּנְבָרֶכְךָ עָלֶיהָ בִּקְדֻשָּׁה וּבְטָהֳרָה. [רְצֵה וְהַחֲלִיצֵנוּ בְּיוֹם הַשַּׁבָּת הַזֶּה, וְ]שַׂמְּחֵנוּ בְּיוֹם חַג הַמַּצּוֹת הַזֶּה. כִּי אַתָּה, יְיָ, טוֹב וּמֵטִיב לַכֹּל, וְנוֹדֶה לְּךָ עַל הָאָרֶץ וְעַל פְּרִי הַגָּפֶן. בָּרוּךְ אַתָּה, יְיָ, עַל הָאָרֶץ וְעַל פְּרִי הַגָּפֶן.

15. Nirtzah — Conclude the Seder. — נרצה

The following verses are from the conclusion of a PIYYUT which enumerated all the regulations of the Seder.

Now is our Seder concluded,
Each custom and law fulfilled;
As we gathered to celebrate a Seder this night,
May we be worthy in freedom next year
Again to celebrate a Seder.

חֲסַל סִדּוּר פֶּסַח כְּהִלְכָתוֹ,
כְּכָל מִשְׁפָּטוֹ וְחֻקָּתוֹ;
כַּאֲשֶׁר זָכִינוּ לְסַדֵּר אוֹתוֹ,
כֵּן נִזְכֶּה לַעֲשׂוֹתוֹ.

O Pure One, who dwellest on high,
Raise up Thy numberless flock,
Speedily lead Thou the shoots of Thy stock
Redeemed, to Zion with song.

זָךְ שׁוֹכֵן מְעוֹנָה,
קוֹמֵם קְהַל עֲדַת מִי מָנָה;
בְּקָרוֹב נַהֵל נִטְעֵי כַנָּה,
פְּדוּיִם לְצִיּוֹן בְּרִנָּה.

לשנה הבאה
בירושלים

LE-SHANAH HA-BA-AH BI-Y'RUSHA-LA-YIM!
NEXT YEAR IN JERUSALEM!

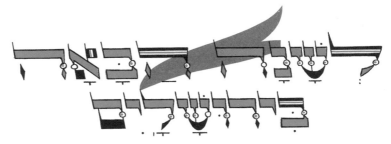

Twice a year we Jews proclaim: "Next year in Jerusalem!"—once at the Seder and again on the Day of Atonement, after the Shofar is sounded at the conclusion of the NEILAH SERVICE. In their centuries of wandering, the affirmation "Next year in Jerusalem!" encouraged the Jews to renew their faith in the restoration of Zion.

IN GRATEFUL SOLIDARITY WITH THE STATE OF ISRAEL

Fill an additional cup of wine. (This cup of wine is optional.)

At the Seder we drink four cups of wine, symbolic of the four verses of redemption mentioned in the Bible. At many Seder observances, these are now followed by a *fifth* verse—commemorating the return, in modern times, of our people to Zion: **וְהֵבֵאתִי** V'HE-VE-TI, "And I will bring you in unto the land that I solemnly vowed to give to Abraham, to Isaac, and to Jacob; and I will give it to you for a heritage . . ." (Ex. 6:8)*

In grateful solidarity with the State of Israel, which, we pray, will forever be established upon justice and truth, let us drink another cup of wine.

בָּרוּךְ אַתָּה יְיָ אֱלֹהֵינוּ מֶלֶךְ הָעוֹלָם בּוֹרֵא פְּרִי הַגָּפֶן׃

בָּרוּךְ אַתָּה, יְיָ אֱלֹהֵינוּ, מֶלֶךְ הָעוֹלָם, בּוֹרֵא פְּרִי הַגָּפֶן.

Baruḥ atta Adonai, eloheynu meleḥ ha-olam, boray p'ri ha-gafen.

Praised be Thou, O Lord our God, King of the Universe, Creator of the Fruit of the Vine.

הוֹדוּ לַייָ כִּי טוֹב כִּי לְעוֹלָם חַסְדּוֹ.

Hodu la-donai kee tov, kee l'olam ḥasdo.

Give thanks unto the Lord for He is good;
His mercy is everlasting.

---

* *Seven* nations conspired to destroy the newly created State of Israel and push its inhabitants into the sea. But they were repulsed—recalling the Biblical verse: "The Lord will cause your enemies that rise up against you, to be routed before you; they shall come out against you one way, but they shall flee before you *seven* ways." (Deut. 28:7)

(What transpired in ERETZ YISRAEL is seen by many believers as evidence of "the Hand of God in history," a modern miracle as impressive as any recorded in the Bible.)

CONCLUDING SEDER SONGS

For centuries, the declaration "Next year in Jerusalem!" marked the formal conclusion of the Seder. But, reluctant to leave the Seder table, later generations added new songs and new hymns. At first, these hymns were similar to the synagogue liturgy of Passover. Later, in order to hold the attention of the children, religious folksongs, madrigals of numbers, and nursery rhymes were included. When printing was introduced, these hymns became part of the Haggadah.

כִּי לוֹ נָאֶה

KEE LO NA-EH: "To Him All Praise is Due"

Kee lo na-eh,	**To God praise belongs;**	כִּי לוֹ נָאֶה,
Kee lo ya-eh.	**To Him it is ever due.**	כִּי לוֹ יָאֶה.
A-dir bim-lu-ḥa,	**Mighty in kingship,**	אַ דִּיר בִּמְלוּכָה,
Ba-ḥur ka-ha-la-ḥa,	**Chosen as of right;**	בָּ חוּר כַּהֲלָכָה,
G'du-dav yom-ru lo:	**To Him His host of angels sing:**	גְּ דוּדָיו יֹאמְרוּ לוֹ:
L'ḥa u-l'ḥa,	**"To Thee, just to Thee,**	לְךָ וּלְךָ,
L'ḥa kee l'ḥa,	**To Thee and to Thee alone;**	לְךָ כִּי לְךָ,
L'ḥa af l'ḥa,	**To Thee, yea, only to Thee,**	לְךָ אַף לְךָ,
L'ḥa Adonai ha-mam-la-ḥa	**To Thee, O Lord, is sovereignty."**	לְךָ יְיָ הַמַּמְלָכָה.
Kee lo na-eh,	**To God praise belongs;**	כִּי לוֹ נָאֶה,
Kee lo ya-eh.	**To Him it is ever due.**	כִּי לוֹ יָאֶה.
Da-gul bim-lu-ḥa,	**Foremost in kingship,**	דָּ גוּל בִּמְלוּכָה,
Ha-dur ka-ha-la-ḥa,	**Glorious as of right;**	הָ דוּר כַּהֲלָכָה,
Va-ti-kav yom-ru lo:	**To Him His faithful sing:**	וָ תִיקָיו יֹאמְרוּ לוֹ:
L'ḥa u-l'ḥa,	**"To Thee, just to Thee,**	לְךָ וּלְךָ,
L'ḥa kee l'ḥa,	**To Thee and to Thee alone;**	לְךָ כִּי לְךָ,

This "Hymn of Praise," in alphabetical acrostic, seeks to magnify and multiply the popularly conceived divine qualities. Of unknown authorship, it was probably composed in the Middle Ages in France or Germany. Some scholars ascribe it to Rabbi Eleazar Ha-Kalir of the eighth century. The Biblical phrases are from Psalms, Job, Deuteronomy, Jeremiah, Chronicles, and Isaiah.

L'ḥa af l'ḥa,	To Thee, yea, only to Thee,	לְךָ אַף לְךָ,
L'ḥa Adonai ha-mam-la-ḥa	To Thee, O Lord, is sovereignty."	לְךָ יְיָ הַמַּמְלָכָה.
Kee lo na-eh,	To God praise belongs;	כִּי לוֹ נָאֶה,
Kee lo ya-eh.	To Him it is ever due.	כִּי לוֹ יָאֶה.
Za-kai bim-lu-ḥa,	All-pure in kingship,	זַ כַּאי בִּמְלוּכָה,
Ḥa-sin ka-ha-la-ḥa,	Powerful as of right;	חָ סִין כַּהֲלָכָה,
Taf-se-rav yom-ru lo:	To Him His courtiers sing:	טַ פְסְרָיו יֹאמְרוּ לוֹ:
L'ḥa u-l'ḥa,	"To Thee, just to Thee,	לְךָ וּלְךָ,
L'ḥa kee l'ḥa,	To Thee and to Thee alone;	לְךָ כִּי לְךָ,
L'ḥa af l'ḥa,	To Thee, yea, only to Thee,	לְךָ אַף לְךָ,
L'ḥa Adonai ha-mam-la-ḥa	To Thee, O Lord, is sovereignty."	לְךָ יְיָ הַמַּמְלָכָה.
Kee lo na-eh,	To God praise belongs;	כִּי לוֹ נָאֶה,
Kee lo ya-eh.	To Him it is ever due.	כִּי לוֹ יָאֶה.
Ya-ḥid bim-lu-ḥa,	One alone in kingship,	יָ חִיד בִּמְלוּכָה,
Ka-bir ka-ha-la-ḥa,	Mighty as of right;	כַּ בִּיר כַּהֲלָכָה,
Li-mu-dav yom-ru lo:	To Him His disciples sing:	לִ מּוּדָיו יֹאמְרוּ לוֹ:
L'ḥa u-l'ḥa,	"To Thee, just to Thee,	לְךָ וּלְךָ,
L'ḥa kee l'ḥa,	To Thee and to Thee alone;	לְךָ כִּי לְךָ,
L'ḥa af l'ḥa,	To Thee, yea, only to Thee,	לְךָ אַף לְךָ,
L'ḥa Adonai ha-mam-la-ḥa	To Thee, O Lord, is sovereignty."	לְךָ יְיָ הַמַּמְלָכָה.
Kee lo na-eh,	To God praise belongs;	כִּי לוֹ נָאֶה,
Kee lo ya-eh.	To Him it is ever due.	כִּי לוֹ יָאֶה.
Mo-shayl bim-lu-ḥa,	Exalted in kingship,	מ וֹשֵׁל בִּמְלוּכָה,
No-ra ka-ha-la-ḥa,	Revered as of right;	נ וֹרָא כַּהֲלָכָה,
S'vi-vav yom-ru lo:	To Him His angels sing:	סְ בִיבָיו יֹאמְרוּ לוֹ:
L'ḥa u-l'ḥa,	"To Thee, just to Thee,	לְךָ וּלְךָ,
L'ḥa kee l'ḥa,	To Thee and to Thee alone;	לְךָ כִּי לְךָ,
L'ḥa af l'ḥa,	To Thee, yea, only to Thee,	לְךָ אַף לְךָ,
L'ḥa Adonai ha-mam-la-ḥa	To Thee, O Lord, is sovereignty."	לְךָ יְיָ הַמַּמְלָכָה.

Kee lo na-eh,	To God praise belongs;	כִּי לוֹ נָאֶה.
Kee lo ya-eh.	To Him it is ever due.	כִּי לוֹ יָאֶה.
A-nav bim-lu-ḥa,	Humble in kingship,	עָ נָו בִּמְלוּכָה,
Po-deh ka-ha-la-ḥa,	Redeeming as of right;	פּ וֹדֶה כַּהֲלָכָה,
Tza-di-kav yom-ru lo:	To Him the righteous sing:	צַ דִּיקָיו יֹאמְרוּ לוֹ:
L'ḥa u-l'ḥa,	"To Thee, just to Thee,	לְךָ וּלְךָ,
L'ḥa kee l'ḥa,	To Thee and to Thee alone;	לְךָ כִּי לְךָ,
L'ḥa af l'ḥa,	To Thee, yea, only to Thee,	לְךָ אַף לְךָ,
L'ḥa Adonai ha-mam-la-ḥa	To Thee, O Lord, is sovereignty."	לְךָ יְיָ הַמַּמְלָכָה.
Kee lo na-eh,	To God praise belongs;	כִּי לוֹ נָאֶה.
Kee lo ya-eh.	To Him it is ever due.	כִּי לוֹ יָאֶה.
Ka-dosh bim-lu-ḥa,	Holy in kingship,	קָ דוֹשׁ בִּמְלוּכָה,
Ra-ḥum ka-ha-la-ḥa,	Merciful as of right;	רַ חוּם כַּהֲלָכָה,
Shin-a-nav yom-ru lo:	To Him His myriad hosts sing:	שִׁ נְאַנָּיו יֹאמְרוּ לוֹ:
L'ḥa u-l'ḥa,	"To Thee, just to Thee,	לְךָ וּלְךָ,
L'ḥa kee l'ḥa,	To Thee and to Thee alone;	לְךָ כִּי לְךָ,
L'ḥa af l'ḥa,	To Thee, yea, only to Thee,	לְךָ אַף לְךָ,
L'ḥa Adonai ha-mam-la-ḥa	To Thee, O Lord, is sovereignty."	לְךָ יְיָ הַמַּמְלָכָה.
Kee lo na-eh,	To God praise belongs;	כִּי לוֹ נָאֶה,
Kee lo ya-eh.	To Him it is ever due.	כִּי לוֹ יָאֶה.
Ta-kif bim-lu-ḥa,	All-powerful in kingship,	תַּ קִּיף בִּמְלוּכָה,
To-mayḥ ka-ha-la-ḥa,	Sustaining as of right;	תּ וֹמֵךְ כַּהֲלָכָה,
T'mi-mav yom-ru lo:	To Him the upright sing:	תְּמִימָיו יֹאמְרוּ לוֹ:
L'ḥa u-l'ḥa,	"To Thee, just to Thee,	לְךָ וּלְךָ,
L'ḥa kee l'ha,	To Thee and to Thee alone;	לְךָ כִּי לְךָ,
L'ḥa af l'ḥa,	To Thee, yea, only to Thee,	לְךָ אַף לְךָ,
L'ḥa Adonai ha-mam-la-ḥa	To Thee, O Lord, is sovereignty."	לְךָ יְיָ הַמַּמְלָכָה.
Kee lo na-eh,	To God praise belongs;	כִּי לוֹ נָאֶה,
Kee lo ya-eh.	To Him it is ever due.	כִּי לוֹ יָאֶה.

אַדִּיר הוּא

ADDIR HU

A-dir hu, a-dir hu,	Mighty is He! Mighty is He!	אַ דִּיר הוּא, אַדִּיר הוּא,
Yiv-neh vay-to b'karov.	May He build His Temple soon.	יִבְנֶה בֵיתוֹ בְּקָרוֹב,
Bim-hay-ra, bim-hay-ra,	Speedily, speedily,	בִּמְהֵרָה בִּמְהֵרָה
B'ya-may-nu b'karov.	In our lifetime may it be.	בְּיָמֵינוּ בְּקָרוֹב,
Eyl b'nay, Eyl b'nay,	Build, O Lord! Build, O Lord!	אֵל בְּנֵה, אֵל בְּנֵה!
B'nay vayt-ḥa b'karov.	Build Thy Temple speedily!	בְּנֵה בֵיתְךָ בְּקָרוֹב!
Ba-ḥur hu, ga-dol hu,	Chosen, great,	בָּ חוּר הוּא, גָּ דוֹל הוּא,
Da-gul hu,	renowned is He!	דָּ גוּל הוּא,
Yiv-neh vay-to b'karov.	May He build His Temple soon.	יִבְנֶה בֵיתוֹ בְּקָרוֹב.
Bim-hay-ra, bim-hay-ra,	Speedily, speedily,	בִּמְהֵרָה בִּמְהֵרָה
B'ya-may-nu b'karov.	In our lifetime may it be.	בְּיָמֵינוּ בְּקָרוֹב,
Eyl b'nay, Eyl b'nay,	Build, O Lord! Build, O Lord!	אֵל בְּנֵה, אֵל בְּנֵה!
B'nay vayt-ḥa b'karov.	Build Thy Temple speedily!	בְּנֵה בֵיתְךָ בְּקָרוֹב!
Ha-dur hu, va-tik hu,	Glorious, faithful,	הָ דוּר הוּא, וָ תִיק הוּא,
Za-kai hu,	pure is He!	זַ כַּאי הוּא,
Yiv-neh vay-to b'karov.	May He build His Temple soon.	יִבְנֶה בֵיתוֹ בְּקָרוֹב,
Bim-hay-ra, bim-hay-ra,	Speedily, speedily,	בִּמְהֵרָה בִּמְהֵרָה
B'ya-may-nu b'karov.	In our lifetime may it be.	בְּיָמֵינוּ בְּקָרוֹב,
Eyl b'nay, Eyl b'nay,	Build, O Lord! Build, O Lord!	אֵל בְּנֵה, אֵל בְּנֵה!
B'nay vayt-ḥa b'karov.	Build Thy Temple speedily!	בְּנֵה בֵיתְךָ בְּקָרוֹב!
Ḥa-sid hu, ta-hor hu,	Righteous, faultless,	חָ סִיד הוּא, טָ הוֹר הוּא,
Ya-ḥid hu,	One is He!	יָ חִיד הוּא,
Yiv-neh vay-to b'karov.	May He build His Temple soon.	יִבְנֶה בֵיתוֹ בְּקָרוֹב,
Bim-hay-ra, bim-hay-ra,	Speedily, speedily,	בִּמְהֵרָה בִּמְהֵרָה
B'ya-may-nu b'karov.	In our lifetime may it be.	בְּיָמֵינוּ בְּקָרוֹב,

The twin themes of this anonymous alphabetical acrostic are the greatness of God and the hope for the speedy restoration of Zion (as symbolized by the rebuilding of the Temple). The first stanza speaks of God as *Adir* (Mighty), while subsequent stanzas introduce additional divine attributes. Each stanza concludes with the refrain: "Build Thy Temple speedily."

Eyl b'nay, Eyl b'nay,	Build, O Lord! Build, O Lord!	אֵל בְּנֵה, אֵל בְּנֵה!
B'nay vayt-ḥa b'karov.	Build Thy Temple speedily!	בְּנֵה בֵיתְךָ בְּקָרוֹב!
Ka-bir hu, la-mud hu,	Mighty, wise and	כַּ בִּיר הוּא, לָ מוּד הוּא,
Me-leḥ hu,	King is He!	מֶ לֶךְ הוּא,
Yiv-neh vay-to b'karov.	May He build His Temple soon.	יִבְנֶה בֵיתוֹ בְּקָרוֹב,
Bim-hay-ra, bim-hay-ra,	Speedily, speedily,	בִּמְהֵרָה בִּמְהֵרָה
B'ya-may-nu b'karov.	In our lifetime may it be.	בְּיָמֵינוּ בְּקָרוֹב,
Eyl b'nay, Eyl b'nay,	Build, O Lord! Build, O Lord!	אֵל בְּנֵה, אֵל בְּנֵה!
B'nay vayt-ḥa b'karov.	Build Thy Temple speedily!	בְּנֵה בֵיתְךָ בְּקָרוֹב!
No-ra hu, sa-giv hu,	Revered, exalted,	נ וֹרָא הוּא, סַ גִּיב הוּא,
Ee-zuz hu,	strong is He!	עִ זּוּז הוּא,
Yiv-neh vay-to b'karov.	May He build His Temple soon.	יִבְנֶה בֵיתוֹ בְּקָרוֹב,
Bim-hay-ra, bim-hay-ra,	Speedily, speedily,	בִּמְהֵרָה בִּמְהֵרָה
B'ya-may-nu b'karov.	In our lifetime may it be.	בְּיָמֵינוּ בְּקָרוֹב,
Eyl b'nay, Eyl b'nay,	Build, O Lord! Build, O Lord!	אֵל בְּנֵה, אֵל בְּנֵה!
B'nay vayt-ḥa b'karov.	Build Thy Temple speedily!	בְּנֵה בֵיתְךָ בְּקָרוֹב!
Po-deh hu, tza-dik hu,	Redeeming, holy,	פּ וֹדֶה הוּא, צַ דִּיק הוּא,
Ka-dosh hu,	just is He!	קָ דוֹשׁ הוּא,
Yiv-neh vay-to b'karov.	May He build His Temple soon.	יִבְנֶה בֵיתוֹ בְּקָרוֹב,
Bim-hay-ra, bim-hay-ra,	Speedily, speedily,	בִּמְהֵרָה בִּמְהֵרָה
B'ya-may-nu b'karov.	In our lifetime may it be.	בְּיָמֵינוּ בְּקָרוֹב,
Eyl b'nay, Eyl b'nay,	Build, O Lord! Build, O Lord!	אֵל בְּנֵה, אֵל בְּנֵה!
B'nay vayt-ḥa b'karov.	Build Thy Temple speedily!	בְּנֵה בֵיתְךָ בְּקָרוֹב!
Ra-ḥum hu, sha-dai hu,	Almighty, merciful	רַ חוּם הוּא, שַׁ דַּי הוּא,
Ta-kif hu,	Lord is He!	תַּ קִּיף הוּא,
Yiv-neh vay-to b'karov.	May He build His Temple soon.	יִבְנֶה בֵיתוֹ בְּקָרוֹב,
Bim-hay-ra, bim-hay-ra,	Speedily, speedily,	בִּמְהֵרָה בִּמְהֵרָה
B'ya-may-nu b'karov.	In our lifetime may it be.	בְּיָמֵינוּ בְּקָרוֹב,
Eyl b'nay, Eyl b'nay,	Build, O Lord! Build, O Lord!	אֵל בְּנֵה, אֵל בְּנֵה!
B'nay vayt-ḥa b'karov.	Build Thy Temple speedily!	בְּנֵה בֵיתְךָ בְּקָרוֹב!

EḤAD MI YODAY-AH: "Who Knows One?" (A Number Madrigal)

E-ḥad mi yo-day-ah?	Who knows the answer to one?	אֶחָד מִי יוֹדֵעַ?
E-ḥad ani yo-day-ah.	I know the answer to one.	אֶחָד אֲנִי יוֹדֵעַ:
E-ḥad Elo-hey-nu	ONE is our God,	אֶחָד אֱלֹהֵינוּ
She-ba-sha-ma-yim u-va-a-retz.	In heaven and on earth.	שֶׁבַּשָּׁמַיִם וּבָאָרֶץ.
Sh'na-yim mi yo-day-ah?	Who knows the answer to two?	שְׁנַיִם מִי יוֹדֵעַ?
Sh'na-yim ani yo-day-ah.	I know the answer to two.	שְׁנַיִם אֲנִי יוֹדֵעַ:
Sh'nay lu-ḥot ha-b'rit,	TWO are Sinai's tablets.	שְׁנֵי לֻחוֹת הַבְּרִית,
E-ḥad Elo-hey-nu	But One alone is our God,	אֶחָד אֱלֹהֵינוּ
She-ba-sha-ma-yim u-va-a-retz.	In heaven and on earth.	שֶׁבַּשָּׁמַיִם וּבָאָרֶץ.
Sh'lo-sha mi yo-day-ah?	Who knows the answer to three?	שְׁלֹשָׁה מִי יוֹדֵעַ?
Sh'lo-sha ani yo-day-ah.	I know the answer to three.	שְׁלֹשָׁה אֲנִי יוֹדֵעַ:
Sh'lo-sha a-vot,	THREE are the patriarch fathers;	שְׁלֹשָׁה אָבוֹת,
Sh'nay lu-ḥot ha-b'rit,	Two are Sinai's tablets.	שְׁנֵי לֻחוֹת הַבְּרִית,
E-ḥad Elo-hey-nu	But One alone is our God,	אֶחָד אֱלֹהֵינוּ
She-ba-sha-ma-yim u-va-a-retz.	In heaven and on earth.	שֶׁבַּשָּׁמַיִם וּבָאָרֶץ.
Ar-ba mi yo-day-ah?	Who knows the answer to four?	אַרְבַּע מִי יוֹדֵעַ?
Ar-ba ani yo-day-ah.	I know the answer to four.	אַרְבַּע אֲנִי יוֹדֵעַ:
Ar-ba ee-ma-hot,	FOUR are the mothers of Israel;	אַרְבַּע אִמָּהוֹת,
Sh'lo-sha a-vot,	Three are the patriarch fathers;	שְׁלֹשָׁה אָבוֹת,
Sh'nay lu-ḥot ha-b'rit,	Two are Sinai's tablets.	שְׁנֵי לֻחוֹת הַבְּרִית,
E-ḥad Elo-hey-nu	But One alone is our God,	אֶחָד אֱלֹהֵינוּ
She-ba-sha-ma-yim u-va-a-retz.	In heaven and on earth.	שֶׁבַּשָּׁמַיִם וּבָאָרֶץ.

"Who Knows One?" is an ancient forerunner of the modern quiz program, designed to stimulate the interest of the children at the Seder. Each of the numbers, from one to thirteen, is associated with an element in the history or beliefs of Judaism.

Other old "number madrigals" invariably stopped at twelve, because thirteen was considered unlucky. But Judaism, frowning upon this superstition, included the number thirteen. (Thirteen is the age of Bar Mitzvah; thirteen are the creeds enumerated by Maimonides; thirteen are the attributes of God. Thirteen is the numerical value of the Hebrew letters in the word EḤAD, which means "ONE," and refers to the unity of God, which is stressed throughout this selection.)

Ḥa-mi-sha mi yo-day-ah?	Who knows the answer to five?	חֲמִשָּׁה מִי יוֹדֵעַ?
Ḥa-mi-sha ani yo-day-ah.	I know the answer to five.	חֲמִשָּׁה אֲנִי יוֹדֵעַ:
Ḥa-mi-sha ḥum-shay to-rah,	FIVE are the Books of Moses;	חֲמִשָּׁה חֻמְשֵׁי תוֹרָה,
Ar-ba ee-ma-hot,	Four are the mothers of Israel;	אַרְבַּע אִמָּהוֹת,
Sh'lo-sha a-vot,	Three are the patriarch fathers;	שְׁלֹשָׁה אָבוֹת,
Sh'nay lu-ḥot ha-b'rit,	Two are Sinai's tablets.	שְׁנֵי לֻחוֹת הַבְּרִית,
E-ḥad Elo-hey-nu	But One alone is our God,	אֶחָד אֱלֹהֵינוּ
She-ba-sha-ma-yim u-va-a-retz.	In heaven and on earth.	שֶׁבַּשָּׁמַיִם וּבָאָרֶץ

Shi-sha mi yo-day-ah?	Who knows the answer to six?	שִׁשָּׁה מִי יוֹדֵעַ?
Shi-sha ani yo-day-ah.	I know the answer to six.	שִׁשָּׁה אֲנִי יוֹדֵעַ:
Shi-sha sid-ray mish-nah,	SIX are the volumes of Mishnah;	שִׁשָּׁה סִדְרֵי מִשְׁנָה,
Ḥa-mi-sha ḥum-shay to-rah,	Five are the Books of Moses;	חֲמִשָּׁה חֻמְשֵׁי תוֹרָה,
Ar-ba ee-ma-hot,	Four are the mothers of Israel:	אַרְבַּע אִמָּהוֹת,
Sh'lo-sha a-vot,	Three are the patriarch fathers;	שְׁלֹשָׁה אָבוֹת,
Sh'nay lu-ḥot ha-b'rit,	Two are Sinai's tablets.	שְׁנֵי לֻחוֹת הַבְּרִית,
E-ḥad Elo-hey-nu	But One alone is our God,	אֶחָד אֱלֹהֵינוּ
She-ba-sha-ma-yim u-va-a-retz.	In heaven and on earth.	שֶׁבַּשָּׁמַיִם וּבָאָרֶץ.

Shiv-ah mi yo-day-ah?	Who knows the answer to seven?	שִׁבְעָה מִי יוֹדֵעַ?
Shiv-ah ani yo-day-ah.	I know the answer to seven.	שִׁבְעָה אֲנִי יוֹדֵעַ:
Shiv-ah ye-may sha-ba-ta,	SEVEN are the days of the week;	שִׁבְעָה יְמֵי שַׁבַּתָּא,
Shi-sha sid-ray mish-nah,	Six are the volumes of Mishnah;	שִׁשָּׁה סִדְרֵי מִשְׁנָה,
Ḥa-mi-sha ḥum-shay to-rah,	Five are the Books of Moses;	חֲמִשָּׁה חֻמְשֵׁי תוֹרָה,
Ar-ba ee-ma-hot,	Four are the mothers of Israel;	אַרְבַּע אִמָּהוֹת,
Sh'lo-sha a-vot,	Three are the patriarch fathers;	שְׁלֹשָׁה אָבוֹת,
Sh'nay lu-ḥot ha-b'rit,	Two are Sinai's tablets.	שְׁנֵי לֻחוֹת הַבְּרִית,
E-ḥad Elo-hey-nu	But One alone is our God,	אֶחָד אֱלֹהֵינוּ
She-ba-sha-ma-yim u-va-a-retz.	In heaven and on earth.	שֶׁבַּשָּׁמַיִם וּבָאָרֶץ.

Sh'mo-na mi yo-day-ah?	Who knows the answer to eight?	שְׁמֹנָה מִי יוֹדֵעַ?
Sh'mo-na ani yo-day-ah.	I know the answer to eight.	שְׁמֹנָה אֲנִי יוֹדֵעַ:
Sh'mo-na ye-may mee-la,	EIGHT are the days to the covenant;*	שְׁמֹנָה יְמֵי מִילָה,
Shiv-ah ye-may sha-ba-ta,	Seven are the days of the week;	שִׁבְעָה יְמֵי שַׁבַּתָּא,
Shi-sha sid-ray mish-nah,	Six are the volumes of Mishnah;	שִׁשָּׁה סִדְרֵי מִשְׁנָה,
Ḥa-mi-sha ḥum-shay to-rah,	Five are the Books of Moses;	חֲמִשָּׁה חֻמְשֵׁי תוֹרָה,
Ar-ba ee-ma-hot,	Four are the mothers of Israel;	אַרְבַּע אִמָּהוֹת,
Sh'lo-sha a-vot,	Three are the patriarch fathers;	שְׁלֹשָׁה אָבוֹת,
Sh'nay lu-ḥot ha-b'rit,	Two are Sinai's tablets.	שְׁנֵי לֻחוֹת הַבְּרִית,
E-ḥad Elo-hey-nu	But One alone is our God,	אֶחָד אֱלֹהֵינוּ
She-ba-sha-ma-yim u-va-a-retz.	In heaven and on earth.	שֶׁבַּשָּׁמַיִם וּבָאָרֶץ.

Tish-ah mi yo-day-ah?	Who knows the answer to nine?	תִּשְׁעָה מִי יוֹדֵעַ?
Tish-ah ani yo-day-ah.	I know the answer to nine.	תִּשְׁעָה אֲנִי יוֹדֵעַ:
Tish-ah yar-ḥay lay-da,	NINE are the months to childbirth;	תִּשְׁעָה יַרְחֵי לֵדָה,
Sh'mo-na ye-may mee-la,	Eight are the days to the covenant;	שְׁמֹנָה יְמֵי מִילָה,
Shiv-ah ye-may sha-ba-ta,	Seven are the days of the week;	שִׁבְעָה יְמֵי שַׁבַּתָּא,
Shi-sha sid-ray mish-nah,	Six are the volumes of Mishnah;	שִׁשָּׁה סִדְרֵי מִשְׁנָה,
Ḥa-mi-sha ḥum-shay to-rah,	Five are the Books of Moses;	חֲמִשָּׁה חֻמְשֵׁי תוֹרָה,
Ar-ba ee-ma-hot,	Four are the mothers of Israel;	אַרְבַּע אִמָּהוֹת,
Sh'lo-sha a-vot,	Three are the patriarch fathers;	שְׁלֹשָׁה אָבוֹת,
Sh'nay lu-ḥot ha-b'rit,	Two are Sinai's tablets.	שְׁנֵי לֻחוֹת הַבְּרִית,
E-ḥad Elo-hey-nu	But One alone is our God,	אֶחָד אֱלֹהֵינוּ
She-ba-sha-ma-yim u-va-a-retz.	In heaven and on earth.	שֶׁבַּשָּׁמַיִם וּבָאָרֶץ.

---

* *B'rit Milah.*

A-sa-ra mi yo-day-ah?	Who knows the answer to ten?	עֲשָׂרָה מִי יוֹדֵעַ?
A-sa-ra ani yo-day-ah.	I know the answer to ten.	עֲשָׂרָה אֲנִי יוֹדֵעַ:
A-sa-ra dib-ra-ya,	TEN are the divine commandments;	עֲשָׂרָה דִבְּרַיָּא,
Tish-ah yar-ḥay lay-da,	Nine are the months to childbirth;	תִּשְׁעָה יַרְחֵי לֵדָה,
Sh'mo-na ye-may mee-la,	Eight are the days to the covenant;	שְׁמֹנָה יְמֵי מִילָה,
Shiv-ah ye-may sha-ba-ta,	Seven are the days of the week;	שִׁבְעָה יְמֵי שַׁבַּתָּא,
Shi-sha sid-ray mish-nah,	Six are the volumes of Mishnah;	שִׁשָּׁה סִדְרֵי מִשְׁנָה,
Ḥa-mi-sha ḥum-shay to-rah,	Five are the Books of Moses;	חֲמִשָּׁה חֻמְשֵׁי תוֹרָה,
Ar-ba ee-ma-hot,	Four are the mothers of Israel;	אַרְבַּע אִמָּהוֹת,
Sh'lo-sha a-vot,	Three are the patriarch fathers;	שְׁלֹשָׁה אָבוֹת,
Sh'nay lu-ḥot ha-b'rit,	Two are Sinai's tablets.	שְׁנֵי לֻחוֹת הַבְּרִית,
E-ḥad Elo-hey-nu	But One alone is our God,	אֶחָד אֱלֹהֵינוּ
She-ba-sha-ma-yim u-va-a-retz.	In heaven and on earth.	שֶׁבַּשָּׁמַיִם וּבָאָרֶץ.

Aḥad a-sar mi yo-day-ah?	Who knows the answer to eleven?	אַחַד עָשָׂר מִי יוֹדֵעַ?
Aḥad a-sar ani yo-day-ah.	I know the answer to eleven.	אַחַד עָשָׂר אֲנִי יוֹדֵעַ:
Aḥad a-sar koḥ-va-ya,	ELEVEN are the stars in Joseph's dream;	אַחַד עָשָׂר כּוֹכְבַיָּא,
A-sa-ra dib-ra-ya,	Ten are the divine commandments;	עֲשָׂרָה דִבְּרַיָּא,
Tish-ah yar-ḥay lay-da,	Nine are the months to childbirth;	תִּשְׁעָה יַרְחֵי לֵדָה,
Sh'mo-na ye-may mee-la,	Eight are the days to the covenant;	שְׁמֹנָה יְמֵי מִילָה,
Shiv-ah ye-may sha-ba-ta,	Seven are the days of the week;	שִׁבְעָה יְמֵי שַׁבַּתָּא,
Shi-sha sid-ray mish-nah,	Six are the volumes of Mishnah;	שִׁשָּׁה סִדְרֵי מִשְׁנָה,
Ḥa-mi-sha ḥum-shay to-rah,	Five are the Books of Moses;	חֲמִשָּׁה חֻמְשֵׁי תוֹרָה,
Ar-ba ee-ma-hot,	Four are the mothers of Israel;	אַרְבַּע אִמָּהוֹת,
Sh'lo-sha a-vot,	Three are the patriarch fathers;	שְׁלֹשָׁה אָבוֹת,
Sh'nay lu-ḥot ha-b'rit,	Two are Sinai's tablets.	שְׁנֵי לֻחוֹת הַבְּרִית,
E-ḥad Elo-hey-nu	But One alone is our God,	אֶחָד אֱלֹהֵינוּ
She-ba-sha-ma-yim u-va-a-retz.	In heaven and on earth.	שֶׁבַּשָּׁמַיִם וּבָאָרֶץ.

Sh'naym a-sar mi yo-day-ah?	Who knows the answer to twelve?	שְׁנֵים עָשָׂר מִי יוֹדֵעַ?
Sh'naym a-sar ani yo-day-ah.	I know the answer to twelve.	שְׁנֵים עָשָׂר אֲנִי יוֹדֵעַ:
Sh'naym a-sar shiv-ta-ya,	TWELVE are the tribes of Israel;	שְׁנֵים עָשָׂר שִׁבְטַיָּא,
Aḥad a-sar koḥ-va-ya,	Eleven are the stars in Joseph's dream;	אַחַד עָשָׂר כּוֹכְבַיָּא,
A-sa-ra dib-ra-ya,	Ten are the divine commandments;	עֲשָׂרָה דִבְּרַיָּא,
Tish-ah yar-ḥay lay-da,	Nine are the months to childbirth;	תִּשְׁעָה יַרְחֵי לֵדָה,
Sh'mo-na ye-may mee-la,	Eight are the days to the covenant;	שְׁמֹנָה יְמֵי מִילָה,
Shiv-ah ye-may sha-ba-ta,	Seven are the days of the week;	שִׁבְעָה יְמֵי שַׁבַּתָּא,
Shi-sha sid-ray mish-nah,	Six are the volumes of Mishnah;	שִׁשָּׁה סִדְרֵי מִשְׁנָה,
Ḥa-mi-sha ḥum-shay to-rah,	Five are the Books of Moses;	חֲמִשָּׁה חֻמְשֵׁי תוֹרָה,
Ar-ba ee-ma-hot,	Four are the mothers of Israel;	אַרְבַּע אִמָּהוֹת,
Sh'lo-sha a-vot,	Three are the patriarch fathers;	שְׁלֹשָׁה אָבוֹת,
Sh'nay lu-ḥot ha-b'rit,	Two are Sinai's tablets.	שְׁנֵי לֻחוֹת הַבְּרִית,
E-ḥad Elo-hey-nu	But One alone is our God,	אֶחָד אֱלֹהֵינוּ
She-ba-sha-ma-yim u-va-a-retz.	In heaven and on earth.	שֶׁבַּשָּׁמַיִם וּבָאָרֶץ.

Sh'lo-sha a-sar mi yo-day-ah?	Who knows the answer to thirteen?	שְׁלֹשָׁה עָשָׂר מִי יוֹדֵעַ?
Sh'lo-sha a-sar ani yo-day-ah.	I know the answer to thirteen.	שְׁלֹשָׁה עָשָׂר אֲנִי יוֹדֵעַ:
Sh'lo-sha a-sar mi-da-ya,	THIRTEEN are the attributes of God;*	שְׁלֹשָׁה עָשָׂר מִדַּיָּא,
Sh'naym a-sar shiv-ta-ya,	Twelve are the tribes of Israel;	שְׁנֵים עָשָׂר שִׁבְטַיָּא,
Aḥad a-sar koḥ-va-ya,	Eleven are the stars in Joseph's dream;	אַחַד עָשָׂר כּוֹכְבַיָּא,
A-sa-ra dib-ra-ya,	Ten are the divine commandments;	עֲשָׂרָה דִבְּרַיָּא,
Tish-ah yar-ḥay lay-da,	Nine are the months to childbirth;	תִּשְׁעָה יַרְחֵי לֵדָה,
Sh'mo-na ye-may mee-la,	Eight are the days to the covenant;	שְׁמֹנָה יְמֵי מִילָה,
Shiv-ah ye-may sha-ba-ta,	Seven are the days of the week;	שִׁבְעָה יְמֵי שַׁבַּתָּא,
Shi-sha sid-ray mish-nah,	Six are the volumes of Mishnah;	שִׁשָּׁה סִדְרֵי מִשְׁנָה,
Ḥa-mi-sha ḥum-shay to-rah,	Five are the Books of Moses;	חֲמִשָּׁה חֻמְשֵׁי תוֹרָה,
Ar-ba ee-ma-hot,	Four are the mothers of Israel;	אַרְבַּע אִמָּהוֹת,
Sh'lo-sha a-vot,	Three are the patriarch fathers;	שְׁלֹשָׁה אָבוֹת,
Sh'nay lu-ḥot ha-b'rit,	Two are Sinai's tablets.	שְׁנֵי לֻחוֹת הַבְּרִית,
E-ḥad Elo-hey-nu	But One alone is our God,	אֶחָד אֱלֹהֵינוּ
She-ba-sha-ma-yim u-va-a-retz.	In heaven and on earth.	שֶׁבַּשָּׁמַיִם וּבָאָרֶץ.

* Exodus 34: 6, 7.

חַד גַּדְיָא

ḤAD GADYA

Written in Aramaic, thus pointing to its ancient origin among the Haggadah's supplementary songs, ḤAD GADYA did not become part of the Haggadah until it was included in the Prague edition of 1590.

Although ḤAD GADYA is similar in style to the folk tales of the Middle Ages, and to such nursery rhymes as "The House that Jack Built," it differs from them in that it teaches a moral lesson. Because the Seder is child-centered and geared to keep the children alert to the very end, ḤAD GADYA may have originally been designed to hold their interest, but noted scholars read significant truths into this song. It voices the concept of divine justice. It intimates that there is retribution in store for all oppressors and that, in the scheme of society and government, everyone is responsible to someone higher, with God supreme above all.

Rabbi Jonathan Eybeschütz and others have interpreted ḤAD GADYA as a hymn to God's providence. God is evident in the history of humanity. Israel (The Kid), redeemed by God from Egypt through Moses and Aaron (the two ZUZIM), succumbs to a mightier empire which, in turn, is defeated by other empires, etc., until God's rule of justice triumphs. The cat is Assyria; the dog, Babylonia; the stick, Persia; the water, Greece; the ox, Rome; the slaughterer, the Moslems; the angel of death, the European nations. The Holy One will finally suppress all tyranny, deliver all His children from oppression, re-establish the principle of justice, and bring about the era of peace for all nations.

The Seder thus ends on a hopeful and joyous note. Through the Seder we keep alive humanity's love of freedom.

ḤAD GADYA

Ḥad gad-ya,	An only kid!	חַד גַּדְיָא,
Ḥad gad-ya,	An only kid!	חַד גַּדְיָא,
Diz-van a-ba bit-ray zu-zay,	My father bought for two zuzim.	דִּזְבַן אַבָּא בִּתְרֵי זוּזֵי;
ḤAD GAD-YA!	*Ḥad Gadya!*	חַד גַּדְיָא, חַד גַּדְיָא!
V'ata shun-ra	Then came a cat	וְאָתָא שׁוּנְרָא
V'aḥal l'gad-ya,	And ate the kid	וְאָכַל לְגַדְיָא,
Diz-van a-ba bit-ray zu-zay,	My father bought for two zuzim.	דִּזְבַן אַבָּא בִּתְרֵי זוּזֵי;
ḤAD GAD-YA!	*Ḥad Gadya!*	חַד גַּדְיָא, חַד גַּדְיָא!
V'ata ḥal-ba	Then came a dog	וְאָתָא כַלְבָּא
V'na-shaḥ l'shun-ra,	And bit the cat	וְנָשַׁךְ לְשׁוּנְרָא,
D'aḥal l'gad-ya,	That ate the kid	דְּאָכַל לְגַדְיָא,
Diz-van a-ba bit-ray zu-zay,	My father bought for two zuzim.	דִּזְבַן אַבָּא בִּתְרֵי זוּזֵי;
ḤAD GAD-YA!	*Ḥad Gadya!*	חַד גַּדְיָא, חַד גַּדְיָא!
V'ata ḥut-ra	Then came a stick	וְאָתָא חוּטְרָא
V'hi-ka l'ḥal-ba,	And beat the dog	וְהִכָּה לְכַלְבָּא,
D'na-shaḥ l'shun-ra,	That bit the cat	דְּנָשַׁךְ לְשׁוּנְרָא,
D'aḥal l'gad-ya,	That ate the kid	דְּאָכַל לְגַדְיָא,
Diz-van a-ba bit-ray zu-zay,	My father bought for two zuzim.	דִּזְבַן אַבָּא בִּתְרֵי זוּזֵי;
ḤAD GAD-YA!	*Ḥad Gadya!*	חַד גַּדְיָא, חַד גַּדְיָא!
V'ata nu-ra	Then came a fire	וְאָתָא נוּרָא
V'sa-raf l'ḥut-ra,	And burned the stick	וְשָׂרַף לְחוּטְרָא,
D'hi-ka l'ḥal-ba,	That beat the dog	דְּהִכָּה לְכַלְבָּא,
D'na-shaḥ l'shun-ra,	That bit the cat	דְּנָשַׁךְ לְשׁוּנְרָא,
D'aḥal l'gad-ya,	That ate the kid	דְּאָכַל לְגַדְיָא,
Diz-van a-ba bit-ray zu-zay,	My father bought for two zuzim.	דִּזְבַן אַבָּא בִּתְרֵי זוּזֵי;
ḤAD GAD-YA!	*Ḥad Gadya!*	חַד גַּדְיָא, חַד גַּדְיָא!

V'ata ma-ya	Then came water	וְאָתָא מַיָּא
V'ḥa-va l'nu-ra,	And quenched the fire	וְכָבָה לְנוּרָא,
D'sa-raf l'ḥut-ra,	That burned the stick	דְּשָׂרַף לְחוּטְרָא,
D'hi-ka l'ḥal-ba,	That beat the dog	דְּהִכָּה לְכַלְבָּא,
D'na-shaḥ l'shun-ra,	That bit the cat	דְּנָשַׁךְ לְשׁוּנְרָא,
D'aḥal l'gad-ya,	That ate the kid	דְּאָכַל לְגַדְיָא,
Diz-van a-ba bit-ray zu-zay,	My father bought for two zuzim.	דִּזְבַן אַבָּא בִּתְרֵי זוּזֵי;
ḤAD GAD-YA!	*Ḥad Gadya!*	חַד גַּדְיָא, חַד גַּדְיָא!

V'ata to-ra	Then came an ox	וְאָתָא תוֹרָא
V'sha-ta l'ma-ya,	And drank the water	וְשָׁתָה לְמַיָּא,
D'ḥa-va l'nu-ra,	That quenched the fire	דְּכָבָה לְנוּרָא,
D'sa-raf l'ḥut-ra,	That burned the stick	דְּשָׂרַף לְחוּטְרָא,
D'hi-ka l'ḥal-ba,	That beat the dog	דְּהִכָּה לְכַלְבָּא,
D'na-shaḥ l'shun-ra,	That bit the cat	דְּנָשַׁךְ לְשׁוּנְרָא,
D'aḥal l'gad-ya,	That ate the kid	דְּאָכַל לְגַדְיָא,
Diz-van a-ba bit-ray zu-zay,	My father bought for two zuzim.	דִּזְבַן אַבָּא בִּתְרֵי זוּזֵי;
ḤAD GAD-YA!	*Ḥad Gadya!*	חַד גַּדְיָא, חַד גַּדְיָא!

V'ata ha-sho-ḥayt	Then came a slaughterer	וְאָתָא הַשּׁוֹחֵט
V'sha-ḥat l'to-ra,	And killed the ox	וְשָׁחַט לְתוֹרָא,
D'sha-ta l'ma-ya,	That drank the water	דְּשָׁתָה לְמַיָּא,
D'ḥa-va l'nu-ra,	That quenched the fire	דְּכָבָה לְנוּרָא,
D'sa-raf l'ḥut-ra,	That burned the stick	דְּשָׂרַף לְחוּטְרָא,
D'hi-ka l'ḥal-ba,	That beat the dog	דְּהִכָּה לְכַלְבָּא,
D'na-shaḥ l'shun-ra,	That bit the cat	דְּנָשַׁךְ לְשׁוּנְרָא,
D'aḥal l'gad-ya,	That ate the kid	דְּאָכַל לְגַדְיָא,
Diz-van a-ba bit-ray zu-zay,	My father bought for two zuzim.	דִּזְבַן אַבָּא בִּתְרֵי זוּזֵי;
ḤAD GAD-YA!	*Ḥad Gadya!*	חַד גַּדְיָא, חַד גַּדְיָא!

V'ata malaḥ ha-ma-vet	Then came the angel of death	וְאָתָא מַלְאַךְ הַמָּוֶת,
V'sha-ḥat la-sho-ḥayt,	And slew the slaughterer	וְשָׁחַט לַשּׁוֹחֵט,
D'sha-ḥat l'to-ra,	Who killed the ox	דְּשָׁחַט לְתוֹרָא,
D'sha-ta l'ma-ya,	That drank the water	דְּשָׁתָה לְמַיָּא,
D'ḥa-va l'nu-ra,	That quenched the fire	דְּכָבָה לְנוּרָא,
D'sa-raf l'ḥut-ra,	That burned the stick	דְּשָׂרַף לְחוּטְרָא,
D'hi-ka l'ḥal-ba,	That beat the dog	דְּהִכָּה לְכַלְבָּא,
D'na-shaḥ l'shun-ra,	That bit the cat	דְּנָשַׁךְ לְשׁוּנְרָא,
D'aḥal l'gad-ya,	That ate the kid	דְּאָכַל לְגַדְיָא,
Diz-van a-ba bit-ray zu-zay,	My father bought for two zuzim.	דְּזַבִּן אַבָּא בִּתְרֵי זוּזֵי;
ḤAD GAD-YA!	*Ḥad Gadya!*	חַד גַּדְיָא, חַד גַּדְיָא!

V'ata ha-ka-dosh ba-ruḥ hu	Then came the Holy One, praised be He,	וְאָתָא הַקָּדוֹשׁ בָּרוּךְ הוּא,
V'sha-ḥat l'malaḥ ha-ma-vet,	And smote the angel of death	וְשָׁחַט לְמַלְאַךְ הַמָּוֶת,
D'sha-ḥat la-sho-ḥayt,	Who slew the slaughterer	דְּשָׁחַט לַשּׁוֹחֵט,
D'sha-ḥat l'to-ra,	Who killed the ox	דְּשָׁחַט לְתוֹרָא,
D'sha-ta l'ma-ya,	That drank the water	דְּשָׁתָה לְמַיָּא,
D'ḥa-va l'nu-ra,	That quenched the fire	דְּכָבָה לְנוּרָא,
D'sa-raf l'ḥut-ra,	That burned the stick	דְּשָׂרַף לְחוּטְרָא,
D'hi-ka l'ḥal-ba,	That beat the dog	דְּהִכָּה לְכַלְבָּא,
D'na-shaḥ l'shun-ra,	That bit the cat	דְּנָשַׁךְ לְשׁוּנְרָא,
D'aḥal l'gad-ya,	That ate the kid	דְּאָכַל לְגַדְיָא,
Diz-van a-ba bit-ray zu-zay,	My father bought for two zuzim.	דְּזַבִּן אַבָּא בִּתְרֵי זוּזֵי;
ḤAD GAD-YA!	*Ḥad Gadya!*	חַד גַּדְיָא, חַד גַּדְיָא!

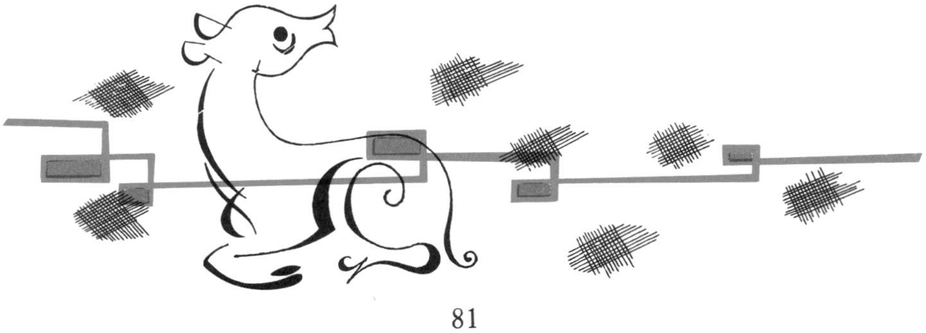

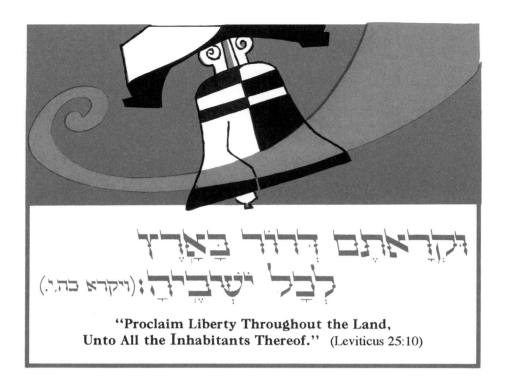

וּקְרָאתֶם דְּרוֹר בָּאָרֶץ
לְכָל יֹשְׁבֶיהָ׃ (ויקרא כה:י)

**"Proclaim Liberty Throughout the Land,
Unto All the Inhabitants Thereof."** (Leviticus 25:10)

"Proclaim Liberty Throughout the Land..."
(Optional Reading)

In the Talmud, this verse is the subject of some lively discussion. One Sage asked: "Are we to proclaim liberty, as the verse implies, only in the Holy Land?" "No!" was the answer. "The Torah requires us to proclaim liberty *everywhere*."

Liberty is indeed universal and indivisible. The world has become a small neighborhood. As long as slavery exists anywhere, liberty is everywhere endangered. There cannot be lasting liberty in one country if there is tyranny in another. The realities of our age, including the prospect of nations claiming control of space, make it imperative for humanity to proclaim liberty everywhere.

But if liberty is to be "proclaimed everywhere," asked another of the Hebrew Sages, "why doesn't the verse specifically state, 'Proclaim liberty throughout *the world*?' Why does the verse say, 'Proclaim liberty throughout the land?' "

The answer is instructive. We must first proclaim liberty in "the land" which is ours, and make it a reality in our own country. It is easy to criticize other nations for discrimination or oppression. We must first put our own house in order, and remove injustice in our own land; then our advocacy of liberty for all peoples will have the ring of sincerity. Moreover, as long as liberty exists in any one country, there is hope that it will spread throughout the world.

Like charity, liberty must begin at home.

Freedom is not a static condition. It is a continuing, democratic process—a dynamic force dedicated to a sublime purpose. That purpose is to translate into daily life the sacred principle that *all* ". . . are endowed by their Creator with certain inalienable rights, that among these are life, liberty and the pursuit of happiness."

CLOSING PRAYER: The Memories of this Night...

Our God and God of our ancestors, as we bring to a close this Seder, commemorating the exodus of our people from Egyptian bondage, we pray that we may carry with us into daily life the message of freedom emphasized in its symbols and rituals.

May the memories of this night inspire us to cast off our own shackles of intolerance, greed and hatred. May we here resolve to break the chains that fetter our minds and blind us to the glory, beauty and goodness which life offers in such abundance.

Help us to realize that we cannot have freedom for ourselves unless we are willing to give it to others.

Through our daily deeds and devotion, may each of us in our own way, help to liberate all who live in fear, poverty and oppression.

May the light of freedom penetrate into all corners of the world, and lift the darkness of tyranny until tyranny is no more, so that all may be truly free. Amen.

Our fathers' God, to Thee
Author of liberty,
To Thee we sing;
Long may our land be bright,
With freedom's holy light,
Protect us by Thy might,
Great God, our King!

(*America*, 4th Verse)

Hatikvah

כָּל עוֹד בַּלֵּבָב פְּנִימָה. נֶפֶשׁ יְהוּדִי הוֹמִיָּה.
וּלְפַאֲתֵי מִזְרָח קָדִימָה. עַיִן לְצִיּוֹן צוֹפִיָּה:
עוֹד לֹא אָבְדָה תִקְוָתֵנוּ. הַתִּקְוָה בַּת שְׁנוֹת אַלְפַּיִם.
לִהְיוֹת עַם חָפְשִׁי בְּאַרְצֵנוּ. אֶרֶץ צִיּוֹן וִירוּשָׁלָיִם:

Kol od ba-ley-vav p'ni-ma,
Nefesh y'hudi ho-miya.
U-l'fa-atay mizraḥ kadima,
Ayin l'tziyon tzo-fiya.
Od lo avda tikva-taynu,
Ha-tikva bat sh'not alpa-yim,
Li-yot am ḥof-shee b'artzay-nu,
Eretz tziyon vi-ru-sha-la-yim.

LE-SHANAH HA-BA-AH BI-Y'RUSHA-LA-YIM!

BIRKAT HAMAZON: Grace after Meals (SHORT FORM)

(When ten or more are present, include the words in brackets.)

LEADER

Let us say the blessing for our food. רַבּוֹתַי, נְבָרֵךְ.

PARTICIPANTS, AND THEN LEADER

Praised be the name of the Lord from this time forth and forever.

יְהִי שֵׁם יְיָ מְבֹרָךְ מֵעַתָּה וְעַד עוֹלָם.

Y'hee shaym Adonai m'vorah̤ may-atta v'ad olam.

LEADER

With the permission of those present, let us praise Him [our God] of whose bounty we have partaken.

בִּרְשׁוּת מָרָנָן וְרַבּוֹתַי נְבָרֵךְ [אֱלֹהֵינוּ] שֶׁאָכַלְנוּ מִשֶּׁלוֹ.

PARTICIPANTS, THEN LEADER

Praised be He [our God] of whose bounty we have partaken and through whose goodness we live.

בָּרוּךְ [אֱלֹהֵינוּ] שֶׁאָכַלְנוּ מִשֶּׁלוֹ וּבְטוּבוֹ חָיִינוּ.

Baruh̤ [eloheynu] she-ah̤alnu mi-shelo u-v'tuvo h̤a-yinu.

PARTICIPANTS AND LEADER

Praised be He and praised be His name. בָּרוּךְ הוּא וּבָרוּךְ שְׁמוֹ.

Baruh̤ hu u-varuh̤ sh'mo.

Baruh̤ atta Adonai,
eloheynu meleh̤ ha-olam,
ha-zan et ha-olam kulo b'tuvo,
b'h̤ayn b'h̤esed u-v'rah̤amim.
Hu notayn leh̤em l'h̤ol basar
kee l'olam h̤asdo.
U-v'tuvo ha-gadol
tamid lo h̤asar lanu,
v'al yeh̤sar lanu
ma-zone l'olam va-ed,
ba-avur sh'mo ha-gadol.
Kee hu el zan u-m'farnays la-kol,
u-may-tiv la-kol, u-may-h̤in ma-zone
l'h̤ol b'ri-yotav asher bara.
Baruh̤ atta Adonai,
ha-zan et ha-kol.

בָּרוּךְ אַתָּה, יְיָ אֱלֹהֵינוּ, מֶלֶךְ הָעוֹלָם, הַזָּן אֶת הָעוֹלָם כֻּלּוֹ בְּטוּבוֹ, בְּחֵן בְּחֶסֶד וּבְרַחֲמִים. הוּא נוֹתֵן לֶחֶם לְכָל בָּשָׂר, כִּי לְעוֹלָם חַסְדּוֹ. וּבְטוּבוֹ הַגָּדוֹל תָּמִיד לֹא חָסַר לָנוּ, וְאַל יֶחְסַר לָנוּ מָזוֹן לְעוֹלָם וָעֶד בַּעֲבוּר שְׁמוֹ הַגָּדוֹל. כִּי הוּא אֵל זָן וּמְפַרְנֵס לַכֹּל, וּמֵטִיב לַכֹּל, וּמֵכִין מָזוֹן לְכָל בְּרִיּוֹתָיו אֲשֶׁר בָּרָא. בָּרוּךְ אַתָּה, יְיָ, הַזָּן אֶת הַכֹּל.

(Praised be God who by His grace sustains the world. May we never lack sustenance.)

BIRKAT HAMAZON: Grace after Meals (SHORT FORM)

RESPONSIVELY:

Praised be our God of whose bounty we have partaken,
And through whose goodness we live.

> By Your grace and lovingkindness, O Lord,
> You nourish and sustain us.

We thankfully recall our liberation from bondage,
And our heritage of justice and compassion.

> We are grateful for our tradition of Torah,
> Which enriches our lives and ennobles our souls.

Remember in mercy, O Lord, Your people Israel,
Bless Jerusalem, and grant us peace.

> Bless all assembled at this table (these tables).
> Strengthen all who strive for justice and peace.

It is written in the Torah: "When you have eaten and are satisfied, you shall praise the Lord your God for the good land which He has given you." (Deut. 8:10) Praised be Thou, O Lord, for the land and its produce.

כַּכָּתוּב: וְאָכַלְתָּ וְשָׂבָעְתָּ, וּבֵרַכְתָּ אֶת
יְיָ אֱלֹהֶיךָ עַל הָאָרֶץ הַטֹּבָה אֲשֶׁר
נָתַן לָךְ. בָּרוּךְ אַתָּה, יְיָ, עַל הָאָרֶץ
וְעַל הַמָּזוֹן.

Ka-katuv, v'aḥalta v'savata u-vay-raḥta et Adonai elo-heḥa
al ha-aretz ha-tova asher natan laḥ.
Baruḥ atta Adonai, al ha-aretz v'al ha-mazon.

Rebuild Jerusalem, Thy holy city, speedily in our lifetime. Praised be Thou, O Lord, who in Thy mercy rebuildest Jerusalem. Amen.

וּבְנֵה יְרוּשָׁלַיִם עִיר הַקֹּדֶשׁ בִּמְהֵרָה
בְיָמֵינוּ. בָּרוּךְ אַתָּה, יְיָ, בּוֹנֵה בְרַחֲמָיו
יְרוּשָׁלָיִם, אָמֵן.

Uvnay yeru-shala-yim ir ha-kodesh bim-hayra ve-yamaynu.
Baruḥ atta Adonai, boneh ve-raḥamav yeru-shala-yim, amen.

The passages below, each beginning with HA-RAḤAMAN *("May the Merciful One"), are read or chanted by the Leader—or by a participant.*

On Sabbath add:

May the Merciful One find us worthy of the unending Sabbath and serenity of the world to come.

הָרַחֲמָן, הוּא יַנְחִילֵנוּ יוֹם שֶׁכֻּלּוֹ שַׁבָּת וּמְנוּחָה לְחַיֵּי הָעוֹלָמִים.

(Ha-raḥaman, hu yanḥi-laynu yom sheh-kulo shabbat u-m'nuḥa l'ḥa-yay ha-olamim.)

May the Merciful One grant us the day of complete happiness.

הָרַחֲמָן, הוּא יַנְחִילֵנוּ יוֹם שֶׁכֻּלּוֹ טוֹב.

Ha-raḥaman, hu yanḥi-laynu yom sheh-kulo tov.

May the Merciful One bless the State of Israel and shield it from all peril.

הָרַחֲמָן, הוּא יְבָרֵךְ אֶת מְדִינַת יִשְׂרָאֵל וְיָגֵן עָלֶיהָ.

Ha-raḥaman, hu y'va-rayḥ et m'dinat yisrael v'ya-gayn aleha.

May the Merciful One bless the oppressed and afflicted of our people, and lead them from darkness into the light of freedom.

הָרַחֲמָן, הוּא יְבָרֵךְ אֶת אַחֵינוּ הַנְּתוּנִים בְּצָרָה. וְיוֹצִיאֵם מֵאֲפֵלָה לְאוֹרָה, וּמִשִּׁעְבּוּד לִגְאֻלָּה.

Ha-raḥaman, hu y'va-rayḥ et aḥay-nu ha-n'tunim b'tzara, v'yo-tzi-aym may-afayla l'ora, u-mi-shibud li-ge-ula.

May the Merciful One find us worthy of the Messianic era and of the life to come.

הָרַחֲמָן, הוּא יְזַכֵּנוּ לִימוֹת הַמָּשִׁיחַ וּלְחַיֵּי הָעוֹלָם הַבָּא.

Ha-raḥaman, hu y'za-kaynu li-y'mot ha-ma-shiaḥ u-l'ḥa-yay ha-olam ha-ba.

"He is a tower of deliverance to His (chosen) king, and shows kindness to His anointed one, to David and to his descendants forever." (2 Sam. 22:51)

מִגְדּוֹל יְשׁוּעוֹת מַלְכּוֹ וְעֹשֶׂה חֶסֶד לִמְשִׁיחוֹ, לְדָוִד וּלְזַרְעוֹ עַד עוֹלָם.

May the Maker of peace in the heavenly spheres, grant peace to us, and to all Israel, and let us say, Amen.

עֹשֶׂה שָׁלוֹם בִּמְרוֹמָיו, הוּא יַעֲשֶׂה שָׁלוֹם עָלֵינוּ וְעַל כָּל יִשְׂרָאֵל, וְאִמְרוּ אָמֵן.

Migdol y'shuot malko v'oseh ḥesed li-m'shiḥo, l' david u-l'zaro ad olam.

Oseh shalom bi-m'romav, hu ya-a-seh shalom alaynu v'al kol yisrael, v'imru amen.

The Seder continues at the middle of page 43.

THE CUP OF HOPE

Leader fills a special cup of wine, sets it aside, and says:

On this night of sacred memory and joyous celebration,
We call to mind those of our brothers and sisters
Whom this Passover season finds in difficulty and danger.

IN UNISON

Reaffirming our solidarity with our fellow-Jews,
And feeling their anguish in their hour of darkness,
We share the hope of a brighter future.

And pledging our efforts to their just cause,
We recite these words of an ancient prayer,
Asking the blessing of Divine favor
On these and others of our distressed:

הָרַחֲמָן, הוּא יְבָרֵךְ אֶת אַחֵינוּ הַנְּתוּנִים בְּצָרָה.
וְיוֹצִיאֵם מֵאֲפֵלָה לְאוֹרָה, וּמִשִּׁעְבּוּד לִגְאֻלָּה.

Ha-raḥaman, hu y'va-rayḥ et aḥay-nu ha-n'tunim b'tzara,
v'yo-tzi-aym may-afayla l'ora, u-mi-shibud li-ge-ula.

May the Merciful One bless our oppressed and afflicted brethren,
and lead them from darkness into light, from oppression into redemption.

May our prayers strengthen them;
And may our efforts assist them.
May our Cup of Hope sustain them;
And may next Passover find them truly redeemed.

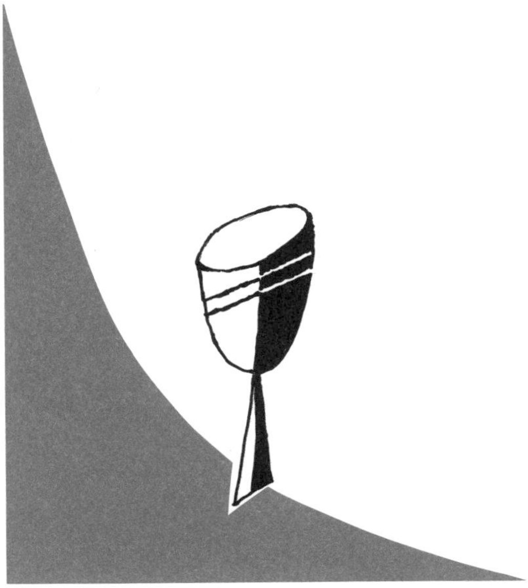

Additional selections may be attached here.